I0818406

STÉPHANE MARIE

A GARDEN TOUR OF FRANCE

Flammarion Silence, ça pousse!

Preface

Out of all the many delightful and surprising gardens that I have encountered in my years as host of the French television show *Silence, ça pousse!*, how could I pick just twenty-seven? Choosing between them was heart-wrenching. In the almost thirty years since the program was first broadcast, France has won back its place of honor among the gardening nations of the world. In the end, this was what guided my choice: I wanted to highlight the wealth and variety of France's gardens, in all their geographical diversity.

France boasts a multitude of splendid parks and gardens. However, what is new today is the creativity and character that can be admired in so many of them.

I have always believed that visiting a garden is also a way of getting to know the personality of those who created it. This tour of France is an introduction not only to beautiful gardens, but also to the remarkable individuals who have often devoted much of their lives to them, so that we can enjoy these oases of greenery.

So, take a stroll through the pages of this book and join me on a journey filled with aesthetic and sensory delights, as I take you to visit my selection of the most extraordinary gardens that France has to offer.

Bon voyage!

Stéphane Marie

Contents

Burgundy and Franche-Comté

Jardins Aquatiques d'Acorus, Autoreille • Haute-Saône

JARDINS Aquatiques d'ACORUS

✡ Autoreille, Haute-Saône

This nursery selling aquatic plants, including many varieties of water lily, has gradually turned into a magnificent water garden. Its pools and streams are laid out in a valley on the fringes of woodland, with the influence of Japanese gardens never far away—a space conducive to free-flowing ideas.

Back in the 1960s, this pretty village with an unusual name, equidistant from Besançon and Vesoul, already offered a haven of peace from the hustle and bustle of daily life, with its clusters of tile-roofed houses in a bucolic setting. For many years now, it has also been home to Sylvie and Olivier Benoist, and the location of the peaceful oasis they have created to soothe the soul and the world.

Sylvie was a geneticist by profession, Olivier a computer engineer. City-dwellers, they both loved nature and were drawn to it, especially to water. In the early 1990s, they left the urban environment and their hectic lives behind and moved to an old farm in Franche-Comté, a region dear to them both.

Their dream quickly began to take shape, and they formed a plan to transform the seven and a half acres (three hectares) of rolling land into a landscape garden. Wholly absorbed by their passion, they little suspected the scale of the task that awaited them. As promising as it might have looked, however, this stretch of grazing land lacked one distinctive feature: it was absolutely devoid of any source of water, an awkward "detail" when your ambition is to revive the concept of the water garden—former examples of which are now largely neglected and in a poor state of preservation—to its former glory.

Undeterred, they armed themselves with spades (resources being limited at the time) and valiantly set about shaping their domain. Working against the natural

slope of the land, they built up earth embankments to form ponds, then added waterfalls, streams, rockeries, and terraces around them, with a system of water pumps to supply all the different features in a perpetual loop.

The Acorus water gardens evolved over a period of thirty years, as the couple embellished the edges of the water features with planting schemes of Japanese inspiration. In the meantime, they opened up a nursery selling aquatic plants—a rarity at the time—and hired out their skills as pond designers, with the gardens serving as their testing ground, showcase, and nursery. By the sweat of their brows and over many years, they have accomplished a herculean task, and created the delightful gardens that we can now enjoy at our leisure.

Entry to the garden is through a scarlet-and-purple *torii* reminiscent of the Japanese gardens at Maulévrier (see p. 224). These ornamental gateways to Japanese temples mark the transition from the mundane to the sacred, or, more prosaically, to a space of tranquility. The gardens boast eighteen different zones, which include the Chemin des Écorces (Bark Path), Jardin Zen (Zen Garden), Bassins en Cascades (Waterfall Pond), Arbres en Nuages (Cloud Trees), and Massif 3 Pins (Three Pines), along with the winter garden, the stream, and the conservatory housing clipped maples and pines. Everywhere, benches invite you to sit, look, and listen. For Olivier Benoist, this is where the secret lies: forget your watch and mobile phone, and allow yourself to gaze in wonder at the toads, dragonflies, salamanders, and newts that populate this mysterious land of water lilies and giant lotus flowers.

Between bamboo groves and niwaki—garden trees—pruned into cloud shapes, visitors come upon wooden sculptures by the artist Dominique Calame, who also created the entrance gate. Wooden pontoons and footbridges span the water features, some leading to ponds with a wilder look, like natural features in the countryside. The Benoists never tire of admiring the biodiversity that they have nurtured and learned to appreciate through their work.

A lot of the Japanese ambience emanates from the ponds, where the couple grow the water lilies and lotuses whose languid beauty first seduced them. Of the countless varieties of water lily, some bear flowers resembling dahlias or peonies, with petals that may be round, pointed, or even crimped, covering the surface of the water with exotic blooms in shades of blue, purple, and pink. Around them float the intriguing apple-green leaves of water lettuce, with purple-leaved colocasias and the towering stems of papyrus.

This slowly unfolding choreography of color continues in harmonious fashion in the chiaroscuro of the landscaping. A weeping willow casts its shade over the waterfall pond: pruned over twenty-seven years, it stands out as a veteran among the "young" Japanese maples, Judas trees, and Tibetan cherry trees. Olivier Benoist attaches great importance to what he refers to as the "borrowed landscape." As visitors climb the gentle slope punctuated with pools that reflect the light and the planting on their banks, the surrounding countryside is drawn into the gardens through the many windows that have been created by patient pruning of the trees to frame new vistas: the tip of the spire of the village church and the trees of the Forêt de Gy rise between the dogwoods, lotus flowers, bamboos, and white water clover flowers.

Rhododendrons, azaleas, geraniums, and asters diffuse their scents and colors over the hillside with the changing seasons. Nowadays, the garden is home to over a thousand varieties of trees, aquatic plants, shrubs, carnivorous plants, perennials, ferns, and grasses. Sylvie Benoist is right when she says, "A gardener is a painter of life," and the composition here is sublime. With the help of their son Johan, a hydrobiologist, Sylvie and Olivier continue their work, planting new trees and shrubs and designing new ponds year after year. It feels as though these extraordinarily tranquil gardens have always been here, and, with their dancing dragonflies and butterflies, their waterfalls, and their water lilies, they offer a welcome escape from the hectic pace of everyday life. •

A vocation for water gardening

The Benoist family loves to share, and this is what they base their business on. The decision to pass on their knowledge of water gardening was made as soon as they planted their very first water lilies. Their nursery sells around two hundred species of aquatic plants, as well as baskets for planting them. More ambitious gardeners will also find tarpaulins or felt, and can obtain generously given expert advice on making a pond.

Practical Information

Jardins Aquatiques d'Acorus
14 Rue des Corvées
70700 Autoreille
Tel.: +33 (0)3 84 32 90 22
jardin-aquatique-acorus@nordnet.fr

Opening Hours

➛ Late March–late October:
Wednesday–Sunday and public holidays:
10 a.m.–12 p.m., 2 p.m.–6 p.m.

➛ Late October–late March:
Annual closure

➛ Guided tours and sale of aquatic plants by appointment.

➛ **jardin-aquatique-acorus.fr** (in French)

Brittany

Jardins de Kerdalo, Trédarzec • Côtes-d'Armor
Jardin de Pellinec, Penvénan • Côtes-d'Armor
Jardins de La Ballue, Bazouges-la-Pérouse • Ille-et-Vilaine

JARDINS de KERDALO

✲ Trédarzec, Côtes-d'Armor

Created from scratch in the 1960s by Prince Peter Wolkonsky, Kerdalo is the masterpiece of a true garden aficionado. Inventive and perfectly proportioned, the gardens feature a wealth of plants showcased in a design that is both rare and original.

Replete with enchantments and surprise encounters, the legendary gardens of Kerdalo lie in the valley of the Jaudy river in the Côtes-d'Armor region, some 2,200 miles (3,500 kilometers) from the winding valley of the Volkony river, in the Russian provinces of Tula and Kaluga. What could possibly connect these two rivers—one at the furthest tip of Brittany, the other south of Moscow? A prince, it turns out, whose life drifted and flowed from one riverbank to the other, from the East to the West.

Prince Wolkonsky was from the ancient Russian princely house of Wolkonsky, whose name is derived from none other than the Volkony river. As a small boy in Saint Petersburg, so the story goes, the prince would sneak under cover of dusk into the kitchen garden of the imperial palace adjoining the Wolkonsky estate.

In 1917, the young man, who had developed an early love of botany, color, and landscape, fled the Revolution. He traveled with his mother to sunnier climes, from the plains of Tuscany to the hills of Provence, and learned to paint the landscapes around them.

Kerdalo is home to over five thousand plant species, including Japanese quince and South African pineapple flowers.

After settling in the Paris region, Wolkonsky created his first garden and became friends with the art patron Charles de Noailles, through whom he became a member of the International Dendrology Society, founded to study and enjoy trees and other woody plants. The only thing now lacking for this great lover of the arts, painting, and gardens was a welcoming spot to call home. He found his corner of paradise and a place to put down his roots in the little commune of Trédarzec, in Brittany, where he acquired forty-four acres (eighteen hectares) of land formed by the steep-sided valley of the Jaudy river, facing the old town of Tréguier. Peter Wolkonsky then set about creating his magnum opus. This was in 1965, and the former farm of Le Verger was about to be transformed into Les Jardins de Kerdalo.

Viewed from above, the valley reveals the full extent of the gardens' ingenuity and richness, as well as the skillful design of their layout—a fragile and authentic living canvas, alternating between long meadows and expansive shady groves; formal spaces *à la française* and wild moorland; Mediterranean terraces and cool, damp paths; forests of gunnera and tree ferns; and an Italian grotto and shell pavilions. A succession of garden rooms is laid out around a canal with a pagoda, water stairs, pools, and ponds.

Hailing from Saint Petersburg, Peter Wolkonsky knew that water was a necessity; the very reason he chose to settle here was because he was aware that the land was

crisscrossed by springs. His intention was to direct and shape the water, just as he molded the earth and sculpted the plants.

Now described as an English landscape garden with Italian influences and exotic inspirations, Kerdalo is home to over five thousand plant species, including rare specimens such as *Acacia pravissima* (Ovens wattle) and the pale green pineapple flowers of the South African eucomis bulb.

In spring, summer, and fall, Wolkonsky the artist worked with distinguished nurserymen, such as the English horticulturalist Harold Hillier, to fill the garden's gentle slopes with combinations of colors and textures that harmonized with the changing seasons. From gold to brown, soft green to silver, or pink to white, a stroll through the painterly tableaux becomes an exquisite sensory experience; each new space transports you to another world, with the childlike sensation of assuming a new identity—perhaps an explorer in an equatorial rainforest, or a botanist searching by moonlight for a *groac'h*, the water sprite of Breton myth and legend. In this magical, secret place, anything seems possible. ●

Iconic heels and the Cherree on the Cake

In 1964—the year before Prince Wolkonsky took possession of his valley—a Breton boy of Egyptian heritage was born. Growing up on Rue de Fécamp in the 12th arrondissement of Paris, the young Christian Louboutin's experience of rivières was largely limited to the long glittering necklaces to be seen at Le Palace nightclub in the 1980s and on stage at the Folies Bergère. But the apprentice shoemaker, who had a great love of gardens, took time out from the excitement of Paris nightlife to study the art of landscape gardening.

While Louboutin was rising to international stardom as a designer of stilettos, Kerdalo suffered the devastating effects of the infamous storms of 1987 and 1999. Taken over and restored by Peter Wolkonsky's daughter Isabelle and her husband Timothy Vaughan, the valley that was so beloved by painters and writers was classed as a "Jardin Remarquable" in 2005, then as a historic monument in 2007.

Nevertheless, this secluded yet vulnerable site, with its large stone farmhouse that had been converted into a gentleman's country house in the seventeenth century, was growing old and faded.

In 2021, Christian Louboutin became the gardens' new owner. Inspired by his Breton roots and his passion for landscape gardens, he was determined to breathe new life into them and restore their color. And who better to do so than the inventor of the famous red-soled shoe?

Since April 2024, the Cherree on the Cake tearoom, set up in a former conservatory, has offered Anglo-Breton pastries served on colorful plates. A team of gardeners led by Tanguy Rabin has renovated the gardens, opening up new vistas and showcasing rare species. The pavilions and the Italian grotto are due to be restored, and a shop stocking books, herbariums, and seeds will delight amateur and professional gardeners alike.

Kerdalo has now been rejuvenated and revived, without losing any of its charm. The heady dream of a Russian prince lives on in this picturesque corner of Brittany.

Practical Information

Jardins de Kerdalo
22220 Trédarzec
Tel.: +33 (0)7 65 16 06 75
lesjardinsdekerdalo@gmail.com

Opening Hours

- Late March–late September:
Sunday and Monday: 2:30 p.m.–6:30 p.m.
Tuesday–Thursday: 10 a.m.–1 p.m., 2:30 p.m.–6:30 p.m.
Friday and Saturday: closed
- May 23–31, June 20–28, and October 1–March 29:
Annual closures

- Final admissions at 11:30 a.m. and 5 p.m.
- Guided tours available every morning by appointment.
- In the event of adverse weather conditions, the gardens may be closed.
- **lesjardinsdekerdalo.com**

JARDIN de PELLINEC

✲ Penvénan,
Côtes-d'Armor

Created twenty-five years ago in an exceptional location, the garden at Pellinec is set around a seventeenth-century house standing at the head of a turquoise cove. Taking visitors on an incredible voyage, it features more than twenty thousand plants, all planted by dedicated gardener Gérard Jean, which have pride of place in this extraordinary universe.

There are days of wind and rain when you hunch under a streaming raincoat; there are days of the dreaded Breton drizzle (fulminating against which is part of the Breton deal with the gods, and with life generally); there are stormy skies of outrageous beauty; there is the wildness of the ocean, mocking our frailties. And then there are moments when time stands still. A veil of mist hangs over the quiet of the cove. The pale sea merges with the hazy horizon. The rocks of low-lying islands just offshore pierce the misty air. Two boats skim the tideline. Overhanging the shore, huge exotic leaves rise in dazzling splashes of yellow and brown, gray-green and emerald against the monochrome of the landscape. A dream-like, painterly scene, and a moment in the life of the gardens at Pellinec.

This improbably beautiful spot at Penvénan in north-western Brittany is an extension of the Pink Granite Coast. Sheltered by rolling countryside a little way back from the sea, the estate has been shaped into its present state of perfection by Gérard Jean, its owner and creator, over the past twenty-five years. Dedicated enthusiasts who create outstanding gardens often reach a point in their lives when they resolve to reject the pressures of modern, urban life and the challenge of living in concrete cities, turning their backs on it all, eager to reinvent the concept of time. To these impassioned guardians of an overheated planet and our overheated lives, we owe a huge debt of gratitude for their enthusiasm and their courage.

A former advertising executive, Gérard Jean was all too familiar with the rat race and the hectic pace of city life, to the point of worrying that they were affecting his health. As a boy, growing radishes had been a source of wonder. As he grew older, he never forgot the curious little boy he had once been, and he vowed that he would one day have a garden. In 1993, the Pellinec estate was in a state of abandonment. Obsessed by his dream of a garden and seduced by the seventeen-acre (seven-hectare) site and its idyllic setting, Jean acquired the estate without giving a second thought to the decrepit state of the house.

It was not until a few months later, after clearing the land, leveling the ground, and unearthing buried paths, that he turned his attention to the neglected building. While it was a mere shadow of its former incarnation as a summer camp, it turned out to have originally been a stone-built manor house dating from the reign of Louis XIV. After eighteen months of restoration work, it was brought back to life. Now listed as a historic monument, it has recently been opened to the public.

The design of the gardens has taken shape over many years, inspired by Jean's fertile imagination and perfectionism. Spread over ten acres (four hectares), eight spaces with different themes now unfold in all their splendor, doubtless to be followed by more in the future.

The Jardin Exotique (Exotic Garden) occupies the site of the original kitchen garden of the manor house. Of the vestiges that remained, Jean kept only an enormous *Trachycarpus fortunei*, a hundred-year-old palm tree that inspired the subtropical theme. A long, paved path tempts visitors to stroll among a luxuriant and hugely varied collection of species, including more palms, phormiums, and *Cordyline australis*, with long, pointed leaves in shades of yellow, pink, purple, and even black.

The Jardin Anglais (English Garden) brings a complete change of atmosphere. Looking out to sea, it features winding paths rather than straight lines, and cool lawns instead of clipped box. To provide shelter from the sea spray and wind, Jean planted an evergreen screen below it, backed up by a second row of hardy perennials such as agapanthus and hemerocallis. Island beds of magnolias, rhododendrons, azaleas, and hydrangeas in an infinitely nuanced palette punctuate the one and a quarter acres (half a hectare) of lawn. Jean has worked tirelessly on the design and atmosphere of the gardens, planting nearly 20,000 plants of over 2,450 varieties in the last twenty years.

The water lily pond was an original feature that Jean found on the relevant section of the Cassini Map of France—the first complete map of France, drawn up in the eighteenth century and still used by historians to this day. Having rediscovered its existence on paper, he excavated the site and dug the pond again, to a depth of just over two feet six inches (eighty centimeters) to allow water lilies to flourish. Water irises raise their graceful flowers around them, while astilbes and yellow marsh marigoldsline the banks beneath giant gunnera leaves. The charm of this water feature is also a moving tribute by Gérard Jean to Claude Monet's water lily pond at Giverny.

Island beds of magnolias, rhododendrons, azaleas, and hydrangeas punctuate a verdant green setting.

In the marshy area—now a little less boggy—lies the Japanese iris garden. Here, Jean, who adores this species of over five hundred varieties, was at pains to work out the most elegant way to showcase its beautiful flowers, with their broad, flat petals. So they could be appreciated at close quarters, he built a walkway of duckboards on stilts. With dry feet and heads in the clouds, we can gaze at leisure upon the glorious drifts of mauve, white, pink, blue, and deep purple, noticing the stripes and nuances of color on the petals. Jean is convinced, moreover, that a comparison of the flowers with contemporary engravings reveals that the historic emblem of the kingdom of France was not the lily, but rather the iris. Associated with the regal iris are native plants such as the royal fern, *Osmunda regalis*, and meadowsweet, together with *Zantedeschia aethiopica* "Green Goddess," an unusual variety of arum with green and white spathes.

Equally remarkable are the Jardin Austral (Australasian Garden), with varieties from southern climes; the Allée Himalayenne (Himalayan Alley), an avenue of Himalayan plants; and the Dune aux Succulentes (Dune of Succulents), a collection of aloes, agaves, and cactus, created in 2023. Stretching in front of the *manoir*, finally, is the dreamy magnolia meadow, with forty-eight varieties of this magnificent tree, dazzling visitors in all their white, pink, and pale yellow splendor. •

Sundays only

♥ *Like all precious things, the gardens at Pellinec are revealed sparingly. Gérard Jean makes a point of preserving his garden and tends it lovingly at all times of day. But Sundays are reserved for the public. Listed as a "Jardin Remarquable" since 2013, Pellinec is well worth the wait.*

Practical Information

Jardin de Pellinec
1 Rue de la Baie de Pellinec
22710 Penvénan
Tel.: +33 (0)6 65 43 92 35
contact@le-jardin-de-pellinec.fr

Opening Hours

- Mid-April–mid-September:
  Sunday: 2 p.m.–6 p.m.
- Mid-September–mid-April:
  Annual closure
- Guided tours available by appointment.
- No parking or restroom facilities available on site, and dogs and strollers are not permitted.
- **le-jardin-de-pellinec.fr** (in French)

JARDINS de LA BALLUE

✵ Bazouges-la-Pérouse, Ille-et-Vilaine

Looking out over the glorious countryside of the Couesnon valley, the château of La Ballue offers thirteen gardens to visitors, each with its own unique character, from baroque, to musical, to theatrical. And when in flower, the wisteria walk is a spectacular sight that should not be missed.

An inspiration for writers including Victor Hugo, Honoré de Balzac, Alfred de Musset, and François-René de Châteaubriand, the château of La Ballue and its gardens are now listed as historic monuments. Standing among the hills and woods between Saint-Malo and Mont-Saint-Michel, the granite building was first constructed in the seventeenth century and has since been remodeled many times. The imposing main body of the château, built in the reign of Louis XIII, is flanked by two wings that frame the main courtyard. The pale façade is embellished with pilasters and mullion windows, while the steep slate roofs feature finely carved dormer windows.

Topiary of all shapes and sizes is clipped not only from box, yew, and hornbeam, as elsewhere, but also—and more unusually—from* Cupressus x leylandii, *holly, privet, and thuja.

Taken over and completely restored in 2005 by Marie-Françoise Mathiot-Mathon, the château now offers five luxury *chambres d'hôtes*. With names including Victor Hugo, Diane, and Perse, all are decorated in shades of red, pale blue, or cream, with tasseled tiebacks, four-poster beds, Louis XV paneling, bespoke fabrics by Pierre Frey, and other elegant touches redolent of the Grand Siècle.

From the windows and the main terrace, visitors can enjoy views of the Couesnon valley, with the river flanked by hedgerows, cultivated fields, and endless shades of green, before feasting their eyes on the remarkable gardens below.

In 1942, these were potato fields. In 1973, following an idea by the publisher Claude Arthaud, the then owner, architects Paul Maymont and François Hébert-Stevens created two Mannerist-inspired gardens separated by a sumptuous wisteria walk. After being abandoned once again, the estate was then taken over by Alain and Marie-Françoise Mathiot-Mathon, who fell in love with these labyrinthine gardens and their use of unusual plants. Topiary of all shapes and sizes is clipped not only from box, yew, and hornbeam, as elsewhere, but also—and more unusually—from *Cupressus* x *leylandii*, holly, privet, and thuja.

By dint of their relentless labors, the new owners have recreated a unique garden that is both classical and Mannerist in inspiration, embellished with modern art and regular installations of contemporary works. But it is also playful in design, with contrasts of light and shadow and unexpected vistas. Passing from tunnels into clearings, from shady groves to green rooms flooded with light, the visitor is taken on a journey that feels like a rite of initiation.

Passing from tunnels into clearings, from shady groves to green rooms flooded with light, the visitor is taken on a journey that feels like a rite of initiation.

Laid out on the terrace, overlooking the wooded countryside, is the formal garden *à la française*, its geometric parterres punctuated with topiary and featuring contemporary sculpture at the center. Wisteria makes another appearance here, covering an astonishing colonnade of yews that encloses the space. On the far side of this purple archway lie thirteen green rooms on different themes, bordered by box and yew hedges or rows of topiary.

One of the garden's most iconic elements is the box maze: a tribute to the classical style, its clipped hedges twist and turn with dizzying complexity. Viewed from above, they resemble an unfinished jigsaw puzzle. The "hornbeam grove with a view," a nod to the literary wordplay of the baroque, also evokes E.M. Forster's *A Room with a View*, with its Tuscan setting. The surrounding landscape is glimpsed through a curtain of trees. Via an archway of white wisteria, you reach a grove of the evergreen ferns that grow so prolifically in the region, its shade offering a spot for a welcome rest.

At the center of the scented grove is an octagonal pond with fragrant water lilies. Clipped ogive arches and triangles frame fragrant potted plants, jasmine, and honeysuckle. The green open-air theater, with its yew walls, four lateral frameworks, and grassy stage, hosts summer concerts, often featuring baroque music.

Gently leading back to the château is an avenue of lime trees clipped to form a narrow arcade seventy-six yards (seventy meters) long—a chiaroscuro passage between the light-filled valley and the imposing château. If you are lucky enough to be staying the night, it will be time to take a dip in the pool or try out the spa. Otherwise, a tearoom among the roses and jasmine offers comforting homemade pastries, while the book section in the adjacent shop offers volumes on art and gardens. •

Music at the château

♥ *For several years now, in the summer months, the BarokOpéra collective has been invited to perform music from baroque opera in the gardens of the château. The music of Offenbach, Purcell, and Mozart have all been heard floating through the elegant gardens and groves of this historic château.*

Practical Information

Jardins de La Ballue
Château de La Ballue
35560 Bazouges-la-Pérouse
Tel.: +33 (0)2 99 97 47 86
chateau@la-ballue.com

Opening Hours

- Mid-March–end April:
  Thursday–Sunday: 10 a.m.–6:30 p.m.
- May–September:
  Open daily: 10 a.m.–6:30 p.m.
- October–November 11:
  Thursday–Sunday: 10 a.m.–6:30 p.m.
- November 12–mid-March:
  Annual closure

- Garden also open on public holidays and during special events.
- Guided group tours available by appointment.
- laballuejardin.com/en

Centre and the Loire Valley

Prieuré d'Orsan, Maisonnais • Cher
Château de Valmer, Chançay • Indre-et-Loire
Château du Rivau, Lémeré • Indre-et-Loire
Château de Villandry, Villandry • Indre-et-Loire
Parc Floral d'Apremont, Apremont-sur-Allier • Cher
Château du Lude, Le Lude • Sarthe

PRIEURÉ d'ORSAN

✲ Maisonnais,
Cher

In the late twentieth century, when reinventing the medieval garden was in vogue, the Orsan priory was undeniably one of the most spectacular examples of these recreations. Today it showcases techniques like pleaching and raised wattle beds, some of which had been forgotten to history. Above all, it is a masterly example of the architectural use of plants in a way that is as contemporary as it is medieval.

In the medieval world, the aesthetics of a garden were designed to be appreciated from above, as this human creation was intended for the eyes of the Almighty. Beauty inclined humans toward temptation and pleasure, after all, and from there to sin was but a short step. So it was deemed wiser to avert one's gaze, or rather not to compromise it, and to leave judgement to the divine presence. In the Renaissance period, pleasure became less straitlaced, fortunately, and people were able to give freer rein to their creativity, sometimes at the expense of symbolism.

The Orsan priory bridges the centuries in a unique way, having more or less survived all of the trials and tribulations that have been thrown at it during its long and checkered history. While many of its occupants and visitors down the centuries brought destruction with them, others have made magnificent efforts to restore, reinvent, and maintain the location.

In the twelfth century, Robert d'Arbrissel, founder of the royal abbey of Fontevraud, created a new Fontevrist foundation, the Priory of Notre-Dame d'Orsan, encompassing a chapel, mill, cloister, and numerous convent buildings. At the end of his life, wanting to satisfy the rival demands of the lords of the two sites, d'Arbrissel divided up his mortal remains: his body would go to Fontevraud, while his heart would stay at Orsan. To house the relic, the priory erected a marble mausoleum, which, over the years, became a place of pilgrimage. According to the growing number of pilgrims who flocked there, the relic performed miracles, and Robert d'Arbrissel gained his reputation for saintliness.

Generously endowed by grateful souls and administered with devoted fervor by successive generations of nuns, the priory prospered for centuries. Then came wars and revolution. Having survived the Hundred Years' War, Orsan succumbed to the Wars of Religion. During the French Revolution, the four buildings that were all that remained of the former priory were sold off, and the paneling in the parlor vanished amid the stench of manure and the profiteering of local farmers.

In 1926, the imposing main buildings were, nonetheless, listed as historic monuments. Seventy years later, when chicken coops and dilapidated farm machinery were the sole occupants of the abandoned courtyard overlooked by deserted buildings, architects Patrice Taravella and Sonia Lesot bought the priory and nearly a hundred acres (forty hectares) of surrounding woodland and meadows. They renovated the buildings and conceived a priory constructed from plants, skillfully combining the old with the new, the symbolic with the aesthetic.

Nowadays, whether viewed from above or at ground level, beauty is everywhere to be seen in this space designed for the mind and body—an elegant tribute to the original priory. It was classed as a "Jardin Remarquable" in 2004.

With the help of the scholarly gardener Gilles Guillot, the two architects drew inspiration from medieval illuminations to create twelve enclosed gardens, capturing the essence of the religious order's gardens, at once symbolic and practical.

The visit begins with the cloister, which is devoted to prayer and meditation, as well as being the very first garden, the Garden of Eden. Its grassy paths are flanked by perfectly clipped hornbeam hedges, while drifts of purple alliums and hostas blend softly beside

Albéric
Barbier
NR

them. And in the middle of it all flows a river—or rather a fountain, with jets symbolizing the four rivers that watered Paradise. Squares of vines surround the spring, symbolizing the wine that quenched the thirst of the nuns and the local people, while also symbolizing the Eucharist.

After this the parterres follow quite naturally: the first is planted with spelt, the second with fava beans, with an olive grove nearby. The trio of biblical plants that were used to make bread, wine, and oil thus ensure the health of our bodies and the elevation of our souls. Overlooking the squares is a mesh made up of plants, with windows that to the medieval imagination might have conjured up niches for the twelve apostles.

The maze tempts visitors to linger among the daffodils and crocuses, in search of paradise once again. At the center, an apple tree, clipped to make a flat canopy supported by stakes, provides shade and salvation.

The garden's charm also lies in its unique decorative features: elaborate structures built in situ from chestnut wood, serving as supports for the plants while also embellishing the space with their unexpected airy architecture. Pergolas and edgings in wood, stone, and metal recall medieval techniques, while the hedges are pierced with oval and oeil-de-boeuf windows that offer fresh vistas at every turn. The visit continues with the Jardins de Marie (Mary's Gardens), planted with roses, violets, and lilies—three flowers that are emblematic of the Virgin Mary.

In the large kitchen garden, artichokes, Russian cucumbers, squash, and pumpkins flourish in woven wattle raised beds. The vegetables are mingled with flowers such as red flax, which attracts pollinating insects. The gardener, Thierry Joubert, is a sworn enemy of pesticides and instead favors manual techniques and clever plant combinations. Yet another highlight is the herb garden, dedicated to medicinal plants. Finally, we come to the orchards of pears, apples, and small fruits, all subject to a single rule at Orsan: one fruit is for the birds, the second for visitors, and the third for the owners to make jam.

On the façade of the main building, a large floral heart prompts thoughts of the relic of Robert d'Arbrissel. And so, we come full circle. •

Change of owners

Since 2017, English fashion designers Gareth Casey and Cyril Pearon have been the fortunate new owners of Orsan, breathing new life into the gardens. Inspired by the old spaces, they have created new ones with a focus on respect for nature and plants, always with the aim of making the garden yet more beautiful. A tearoom offers gourmet lunches and teas, and a shop sells a wide range of gardening tools, nesting boxes, fresh fruit juices, and homemade jams.

Practical Information

Prieuré d'Orsan
225 Route d'Orsan
18170 Maisonnais
Tel.: +33 (0)2 48 56 27 50
info@prieuredorsan.com

Opening Hours

➛ Mid-April–early October:
Monday, Wednesday, Thursday, and Friday:
11 a.m.–6 p.m.
Saturday, Sunday, and public holidays:
10 a.m.–7 p.m.
Tuesday: closed

➛ Early October–mid-April:
Annual closure

➛ Final admissions one hour before closing.

➛ **prieuredorsan.com/en**

CHÂTEAU de VALMER

✵ Chançay, Indre-et-Loire

This magnificent walled kitchen garden aspires not to self-sufficiency, but rather to the cultivation of a great diversity of plants from around the globe. Working in conjunction with numerous botanical gardens, it preserves and showcases rare and little-known varieties of fruit and vegetables.

The Valmer domaine has been in the Saint Venant family since 1888, faithfully handed down from one generation to the next. Doubtless encouraged by this historic legacy, the dynasty remains constant and generous in honoring its heritage.

Originally built five centuries ago on the heights above the Brenne valley, the Château de Valmer is said to have belonged to Charles VII. A certain Sieur Binet, counsellor to François I, created a typically Italian Renaissance garden on the rocky spur. Composed of huge terraces with immense retaining walls featuring moldings, the gardens step down the hillside to the canal that lies along its length, dug to the dimensions of the lowest terrace. During this period, in 1524, the astonishing troglodyte chapel was also hollowed out of the volcanic tuff.

The stone gateway and the Pavillon Valmer (Valmer Pavilion) date from the seventeenth century and were designed by Thomas Bonneau, counsellor to Louis XIII. But what of the splendid Renaissance château that had largely survived the depredations of time? In a cruel twist of fate, the main building burned down in 1948, in a fire started accidentally by an iron.

The current owners, the Count and, especially, the Countess de Saint Venant, have compensated for this loss by planting yew walls with openings to precisely replicate the former château's windows and doors. The original railings have survived unscathed, letting visitors admire the garden from this living, green version of the original edifice.

Before exploring the remarkable kitchen garden, visitors should climb up to the heights to appreciate the full beauty of Valmer. Fifty feet (fifteen meters) above the moat, the top terrace offers a breathtaking panorama of the descending terraces,

the grand canal, the valley, and the vineyards of Vouvray. Of the two hundred acres (eighty hectares) of the Valmer estate, eighty-six (thirty-five hectares) are devoted to the vineyards. On the heights, a period weather vane creaks—while it may be unmusical, it still fulfills its valuable function, according to the owner, as an indication of changes in the wind direction.

This terrace also features clipped hornbeam hedges planted in the eighteenth century. They form an indeterminate maze-like design, created for the pleasure of the eyes, for shady walks, or for playing chasing games—not the exclusive prerogative of children, especially in the Age of Enlightenment. Nine species of wild orchid grow here, returning year after year thanks to the cutting of the grass: an example of the emblematic grace of the gardens, where untamed life flourishes, helped along only a little by human hands.

In spring, the Terrasse des Fontaines Florentines (Florentine Fountains Terrace) is fragrant with the scents of tree peonies and "Pierre de Ronsard" roses. But the real stars here are two huge weeping sophora trees, their twisted branches forming extraordinary sculptures. In summer, their long racemes of white flowers cascading down to the moat are truly a beautiful sight to behold. Visitors then climb down to the Terrasse de Léda (Léda's Terrace), walled with clipped hornbeam hedges, recreated by Alix de Saint Venant after an original plan of the gardens that was discovered at the back of an armoire. The splendid circular design of this terrace is faithful to the plan of 1695. A few more steps lead down to a mezzanine level dubbed the Terrasse des Vases d'Anduze (Anduze

But the real stars here are two huge weeping sophora trees, their twisted branches forming extraordinary sculptures.

Vases Terrace), its wall punctuated by tall yew buttresses interspersed with the bright pink panicles of lagerstroemia, or crape myrtle. Finally, flourishing in the moat, with its particular atmospheric conditions of cooler air and dappled sunlight, is a collection of hydrangeas with white and pink flowers and huge velvety leaves.

And now, at last, visitors climb down eighteenth-century steps to the kitchen garden, hidden from view until the last moment and all the more spectacular when it finally appears. To begin with there is the gallery of gourds, consisting of four hundred tropical and subtropical plants and sixty varieties growing under a pergola that stretches for 220 yards (200 meters).

This conservation kitchen garden covering two and a half acres (one hectare) is the crazy yet patiently cultivated creation of Alix de Saint Venant and her gifted gardeners. They began twenty-five years ago with the replanting of the structures: box edging, espaliers, and counter-espaliers for large numbers of fruit trees. They then divided up the four grassy squares and began the active search for heritage vegetables, sourcing them from around the world and from fellow enthusiasts.

Now a member of the Patrimoine Légumier du Centre-Val de Loire association, the garden is home to over a thousand different varieties in many improbable shapes and sizes, including—to name just a few—white carrots, Peruvian ground apple or yacón, tuberous nasturtiums, Peruvian oca, chocolate peppers, edible flowers, and Comtesse de Chambord beans.

Alix de Saint Venant's ambition has always been to cultivate as many different varieties of vegetables and fruit as possible. Through her work in building up this gene bank of heritage plants, this committed landscape gardener views the future as she does the present: in a spirit of sharing. In every era, the most important thing is to feed humanity, to allay people's anxieties by reminding them of the wealth that is available to them, and to inspire their creativity. •

A legend and a host of events

♥ *Listed as a historic monument since 1930 and awarded the "Jardin Remarquable" label in 2004, the estate possesses its share of secrets—not least of which that its walls once concealed a hoard of treasure. In the sixteenth century, a band of marauding Huguenots seized the young daughter of the house. Even when they held her feet to the fire, she remained dignified and silent on the location of the fortune. So, they brought in the village stonemason, who proved more willing to talk. It turned out that the very same stonemason had been summoned to the château a little while earlier, blindfolded, and then ordered to dig out a hiding place in a wall, before filling it in again. And, he added, he had heard pigeons cooing. The Huguenots immediately hotfooted it to the dovecote and made off with the treasure. As a consolation, visitors can always partake in the family mystery "Garden Game," as well as the many other events on offer.*

Practical Information

Château de Valmer
37210 Chançay
Tel.: +33 (0)2 47 52 93 12

Opening Hours

➻ Early January–late April; late September–mid-October; and early November–mid-December (closed November 11), for garden tours by appointment only and sale of wine: Monday–Friday: 10 a.m.–12 p.m., 2 p.m.–4 p.m.

➻ Late April–late September and mid-October–early November: Wednesday–Sunday and public holidays: 2 p.m.–7 p.m.

➻ Les Bons Plan(t)s de Valmer festival held in April: 10 a.m.–6 p.m.

➻ Mid-December–early January: Annual closure

➻ **chateaudevalmer.com/en**

CHÂTEAU du RIVAU

✵ Lémeré,
Indre-et-Loire

This fairy-tale château is surrounded by an equally magical garden. Contemporary art installations have pride of place in the woods, offering an unforgettable experience for young and old alike. Here, nothing is inconsequential, and everything is elegant and refined.

Immense, luminous, and solidly built, this château looks straight out of a fairy tale, under a sky that is often clear, in gentle countryside that stretches to the horizon. Standing on the border between Poitou and Touraine, the château's surrounding land is so fertile that one can imagine its fifteen rainbow gardens have been conjured up magically from the earth.

The dreamy Château de Rivau has belonged to Patricia and Éric Laigneau since 1992. In its time, it has seen kings from Charles VII to François I come and go, along with a Beauvau dynasty, lords and courtiers, warriors and artists, social climbers and dreamers—and Joan of Arc, who in 1429 came to Rivau to equip herself with war horses.

The earliest foundations of the château date back to the thirteenth century. Fortified two hundred years later, it was then modernized during the Renaissance, hence its unique architecture: a fortified castle complete with keep, battlements, and drawbridge, but also open to its gardens and offering all the attractive features—both in its symmetry and its ornamentation—of seventeenth-century architecture. The most ancient of the great châteaux of the Loire Valley and listed as a historic monument since 1918, it still has its royal stables (listed in 1999), tithe barn, and wine press, not to mention its outbuildings, which were once a separate property from the château, at a time when, after surviving centuries of war and turmoil, the estate was virtually abandoned.

Thanks to the determination and talent of the Laigneau family, and twenty-five years of herculean labors on their part, this miraculous spot has been restored to its former glory, blending the old with the new in magnificent fashion.

According to Patricia Laigneau, Rivau is like a child's drawing of a medieval château, a dream from a chivalric romance of knights in shining armor. It was from this, as well as medieval engravings from the archives—themselves the inspiration for many tales—that this landscape architect drew her fairy-tale theme.

The gardens at Rivau have been classed as a "Jardin Remarquable" since 2003. Whatever the month or the season, Patricia ensures that at least two of the gardens are always in bloom. Spread over fifteen acres (six hectares), each has its own name and dominant palette.

In the flower-filled Jardin du Petit Poucet (Tom Thumb Garden), the palette of warm tones is intoxicating. Narcissi and daffodils herald the arrival of spring, closely followed by yellow and orange roses. As summer dawns on the fiery Chemin des Fées (Fairy Path), meanwhile, tulips and *Imperata cylindrica* "Red Baron" turn blood red, rivaling the scarlet roses.

What collection of fairy tales would be complete without the adventures of Alice, lost in the wonderland of the box maze? But first, an essential detour to the Jardin des Philtres d'Amour (Garden of Love Potions), with its many medicinal plants and numerous rose varieties in shades of pink—the color of love (naturally).

Next comes the restrained two-color palette of the Allée des Senteurs (Scented Avenue), carpeted with drifts of white and blue in an English-style planting, with accents of purple alliums. A stroll through the Jardin Secret (Secret Garden) and the heady lavender parterres brings you to La Forêt Qui Court (the Running Forest), where an impressive pair of wooden legs awaits.

One of Rivau's remarkable features is its ability to create a harmonious mix of medieval, Renaissance, and contemporary art, with twenty-two installations scattered through the gardens. Created by well-known artists, they hold great appeal for both adults and children. Everyone feels tiny, floating in a dream world or among the trees of the orchard, in the face of Lilian Bourgeat's seven-league boots: two left feet, left unsold in a shoe shop for giants.

Still feeling minuscule but more daring, we might venture to lean over the rim of a gigantic sake cup, at the bottom of which, according to Japanese tradition, an

erotic image is concealed. Called *After the Rain*, it is a work by Nicole Tran Ba Vang. Art in all its forms can also be found inside the château, from its Renaissance furniture and Gothic fireplaces to the new contemporary works exhibited each year. In the Salle du Festin (Banquet Hall), take time to admire the ceiling fresco by an Italian master, or wander through the Salle du Grand Logis (Great Hall), dedicated to weapons and taxidermy mounts.

It would be almost impossible to leave Rivau without exploring its kitchen garden, worthy of Rabelais's giants Gargantua and Pantagruel—a botanical conservatory of heritage vegetables from the Centre region.

It would be almost impossible to leave Rivau without spending some time in its kitchen garden, worthy of Rabelais's giants Gargantua and Pantagruel—a botanical conservatory of vegetables from the Centre region, including more than fifty species of squash. Rivau's botanical collection of fragrant roses is equally unmissable, with five hundred varieties, making the ultimate love potion in this exceptional garden. In his novel, Rabelais even gave Rivau to one of his captains—just one more mythical figure to have honored the estate, which is perfectly fitting for such a castle of wonders. •

Hotel and restaurants

A four-star hotel on the second floor of the royal stables offers seven sumptuous rooms, each inspired by a major figure from the Renaissance or the Middle Ages, with free access to the gardens in the evening. Following a stroll through the illuminated gardens, guests can choose to dine on the terrace of La Table des Fées, which has been awarded the Green Key International eco-certificate, or at Le Jardin Secret, a restaurant opened more recently in the château courtyard. The ingredients for the elegant dishes at both establishments are locally sourced, naturally. Finally, art exhibitions, activities for children, and themed tours are available to suit all tastes.

Practical Information

Château du Rivau
9 Rue du Château
37120 Lémeré
For general inquiries, group bookings, and the Table des Fées restaurant:
Tel.: +33 (0)2 47 95 77 47
info@chateaudurivau.com

For the hotel:
Tel.: +33 (0)6 62 91 54 43
hotel@chateaudurivau.com

For the Jardin Secret restaurant:
Tel.: +33 (0)6 59 06 86 33
jardinsecretrivau@gmail.com

Opening Hours

➛ April and October–November 11:
Open daily: 10 a.m.–6 p.m.

➛ May–September:
Open daily: 10 a.m.–7 p.m.

➛ November 12–end March:
Annual closure

➛ Final admissions 45 minutes before closing.

➛ **chateaudurivau.com/en**

CHÂTEAU de VILLANDRY

✲ Villandry, Indre-et-Loire

Celebrated for their splendid kitchen gardens, laid out according to those at the Abbey of Saint Gall, the gardens at Villandry are maintained with immaculate care. Few visitors are left unmoved by the sight of the Gardens of Love and of Crosses, with their box hedges clipped in a style inspired by a mix of French, Andalusian, and Moorish gardens.

In the sixteenth century, Jean Breton was the minister of finance under François I, but it was not only for his services to the nation that he would go down in history; he also made a name for himself thanks to his transformation and creation of the Château de Villandry.

Born in Orléans, Breton came from a modest background, but he soon cast off his humble origins by marrying the daughter of the king's then secretary of finance and rapidly gaining both his father-in-law's position and the king's trust. After fighting in Italy, he oversaw the building work at the Château de Chambord, before acquiring the lordship of Colombiers in 1532. Renovated throughout and renamed Villandry, the estate was to become one of the last great Renaissance châteaux of the Loire Valley. Today, Villandry is a UNESCO World Heritage Site.

All that now remains of the original fortress is the keep. Surrounding this are three wings forming a U-shape and a courtyard looking out over the valley of the Cher and Loire rivers. The new concepts of openness, aestheticism, and

pleasure—the guiding principles of the Renaissance—consigned defensive structures and unsophisticated medieval ways to the distant past. Among the many architectural embellishments that became popular were mullion windows, carved pilasters, and arcaded galleries.

The life of the château over the following centuries was checkered. Remodeled, embellished, neglected, and eventually threatened with demolition, it was saved in extremis when it was bought in 1906 by Joachim Carvallo.

Initially overwhelmed by the scale of the task, this brilliant Spanish-born doctor dedicated the rest of his life to Villandry, restoring the château to its original appearance and recreating thc gardens from historical plans and documents. From medieval and Renaissance styles to formal gardens *à la française* and finally English landscape gardens, they now combine all of these different inspirations. A stroll through the gardens at Villandry is a journey through space and time, a deep dive into the history of French garden design crossed with Andalusian and Moorish influences. Restored and rejuvenated by Joachim's great-grandson Henri Carvallo, there are now seven spaces encompassing various themes, covering fifteen acres (six hectares) and arranged over four terraces.

The Jardin d'Ornement (Ornamental Garden), or the Jardin d'Amour and Jardin des Croix (Gardens of Love and of Crosses), created in the early twentieth century with the aid of a Spanish artist and a Spanish landscape architect, present an impressive spectacle from above, with a dazzling tableau of squares planted in intricate patterns. Every facet of love is depicted here. Tender love is symbolized by hearts and flames, while passionate love is represented by broken hearts, endangered by their own passion. Fickle love is portrayed by four fans and horns, depicting unfortunate cuckolded lovers who are not only betrayed but also mocked into the bargain.

In spring, tulips and forget-me-nots bloom among the clipped yew hedges, adding color to this wistful but nonetheless exhilarating design. Soon they will be replaced by begonias, blooming continuously throughout the summer in yellow, red, and white.

By contrast, no flowers are allowed in the Jardin d'Eau (Water Garden), where greenery and fountains create an air of restraint and calm. A large, mirror-like pool, set amid immaculate lawns, is flanked by four basins; here serenity is the watchword.

Villandry has its maze, naturally, inspired by the medieval model. While in Greek mythology the labyrinth led to death, in the Middle Ages it represented the twists and turns of life, eventually leading to personal fulfillment—a route well worth exploring between its geometric hornbeam hedges. You may even be lucky enough to find the shortcut to the central belvedere.

However long your quest takes, light awaits you at the end of the path. The Jardin du Soleil (Sun Garden)—created in 2008 but planned much earlier by Joachim Carvallo—offers three poetic, playful, and contemporary spaces: the Chambre du Soleil (Sun Chamber), Chambre des Nuages (Cloud Chamber), and Chambre des Enfants (Children's Chamber). A pond in the shape of a radiant sun forms the centerpiece of the first; small grassy paths forming triangles weave through the second; outdoor games and decorative apple trees lend enchantment to the third. All three are brimming with roses, shrubs, and perennials chosen for their irresistible appeal to insects. The pollen-bearing plants attract myriad butterflies, bees, and ladybugs, while flocks of birds frolic on the eight-pointed surround of the pond, earning the gardens LPO (League for the Protection of Birds) certification.

Finally, amid all of these magnificent spaces, we come to the Potager d'Ornement (Ornamental Kitchen Garden): the essential centerpiece of Joachim Carvallo's design. Paying homage to the art of garden design, it is also a stylistic continuation of the architecture of the château, set in an enclosed quadrangle bordered by three terraces, like a cloister. Each of its nine parterres contains its own geometric pattern traced in box hedges, and is planted with a mix of vegetables, fruit trees, and flowers. Rare varieties of pears and apples grow together with standard roses, daffodils, tulips, Batavia lettuces, eggplants, fava beans, and a multitude of other species, offering a kaleidoscope of color. The art of these gardens, with all their subtlety and sophistication, is above all a celebration of life. •

Open all year

♥ *Villandry is one of the few major gardens in France that welcomes visitors all year round. As Henri Carvallo says, every visitor is its patron and supporter. The Rendez-Vous aux Jardins takes place in June, with a variety of activities that serve as a reminder of the importance of preserving the gardens. In August, the Nuits de Mille Feux (Nights of a Thousand Lights) showcases Villandry illuminated by two thousand candles, with entertainment and a fireworks display as the grand finale. And on European Heritage Days in September, skilled upholsterers and decorators, stone carvers, cabinetmakers, and other artisans involved in the maintenance of the château are on hand to meet the public.*

Practical Information

Château de Villandry
3 Rue Principale
37510 Villandry
Tel.: +33 (0)2 47 50 02 09
info@chateaudevillandry.com

Opening Hours

Open daily throughout the year (including public holidays, except December 25):

➻ January–February:
9 a.m.–5 p.m. (5:30 p.m. from second week of February)

➻ March–September:
9 a.m.–7 p.m. (6 p.m. in March)

➻ Beginning October–late October:
9 a.m.–6:30 p.m.

➻ Late October–end November:
9 a.m.–5:30 p.m. (5 p.m. from mid-November)

➻ December:
9:30 a.m.–5:30 p.m.

➻ Check website for more details.

➻ Final admissions 30 minutes before closing.

➻ **chateauvillandry.fr**

PARC Floral d'APREMONT

✵ Apremont-sur-Allier, Cher

Created fifty years ago by Gilles de Brissac, the floral garden at Apremont is unique in the way it embraces its surrounding landscape so completely. Charm and imagination are omnipresent here, from the unexpected follies in the park to the pretty village of Apremont itself, which in turn transforms into a blooming garden.

Anyone who relishes the gentle melancholy of nostalgia will be bound to succumb to the charms of the floral park of Apremont. Here, the village, château, and gardens are dedicated to all those who mourn the loss of a rural way of life that is fast disappearing.

The village, home to a population of just seventy, looks as if it has emerged from a fairy tale. Which is very nearly true, since its houses, with their golden stone and ocher tiles, date from the medieval period, a golden age of myth and legend. Roses and wisterias festoon the house walls, and gardens brimming with lavender, hydrangeas, and peonies, box hedges, and vegetable gardens filled with flowers offer a tempting foretaste of the nearby park. The surrounding Berry countryside is similarly lacking in signs of the modern world, with Charolais cattle and sheep grazing beside the still waters of ponds, trees punctuating the horizon here and there, meadows unfolding down the hillsides, and the Allier river flowing placidly through the hamlet and into the Loire at their confluence three miles (five kilometers) downstream. Visitors may pinch themselves, but they are not dreaming: in this special corner near the border of the Berry region, Apremont-sur-Allier has contrived to resist all the onslaughts of the twenty-first century.

All these lovers of beauty are attracted not only by the village and the fifteenth-century château, but also—and perhaps even more so—by the work of Gilles de Brissac, and the splendor and tranquility of the floral garden he has created.

Some of the village houses have been converted into *gîtes* and *chambres d'hôtes* to accommodate the many visitors to the area: an agreeable if slightly incongruous reminder of the permanently connected wider world. All these lovers of beauty are attracted not only by the village and the fifteenth-century château, with is pepperpot towers and arrow-slits, but also—and perhaps even more so—by

the work of Gilles de Brissac, a landscape architect descended from a long line of châtelains of Apremont, and the splendor and tranquility of the floral garden he has created.

It was in the 1970s that Gilles de Brissac decided to create a floral park adjacent to the village. Undeterred by any obstacles, he excavated a lake on the higher land to supply the garden's water features and he had nearly 900 tons (800 tonnes) of stone transported here to build a waterfall. For this was a site that was devoid not only of any features but also—with the exception of four limes—of any trees.

Once the initial groundwork had been completed, he designed an English-style landscape garden over twelve acres (five hectares), structured by formal lines *à la française* and dotted with exotic follies evoking distant lands, of the type that were the height of fashion during the Enlightenment: an expression of Gilles de Brissac's personal whimsies as well as a tribute to the past.

This scented tour begins in the Jardin Blanc (White Garden), inspired by its famous English namesake at Sissinghurst in Kent. Velvety lawns flank the last houses on the edge of the village; a hedge of hornbeams clipped into cones fringes a mixed border in shades of white, silver, gray, and green. As the seasons change, old roses, clematis, hydrangeas, and peonies rise in creamy clouds beneath the famous lime trees, whose dappled shade guides the visitor to the avenue of *Wisteria sinensis* and *W. japonica*. In spring, says Louise Hurstel, heiress to the château, it becomes a spectacular, fragrant canopy of mauve, white, and pink.

The large arboretum pays discreet homage to the botanical collections of the eighteenth and nineteenth centuries with a wide diversity of trees from Europe and around the world, including weeping beeches, *Ginkgo biloba*, bald cypresses (so-called because they drop their leaves early in the season), Japanese maples, and American tulip trees (*Liriodendron tulipifera*), among many others. Hedges separate lawns fringed with spring and summer borders in a changing palette, with successive flowerings of delphiniums, peonies, irises, alliums, and dahlias following pansies and tulips in spring.

The park's three follies stand aloof from the spectacle, spanning a water feature and crowning an eminence. The most famous and oldest is the Pont Chinois (Chinese Bridge), built in 1985. Constructed in wood and steel, painted scarlet, and topped with a pagoda, it spans a pool fringed by bamboos, magnolias, and azaleas. From China, stepping stones lead to the Pavillon Turc (Turkish Pavilion). This pretty building seems to float on the water and, beneath its slate cupola, it is embellished with wrought-iron flowers. With your eyes half-closed, you could almost be on the banks of the Bosphorus. Within it are four paintings by Jacques Roubinet depicting the stages of life through the seasons of the year.

After this Ottoman interlude, visitors can climb up the hill to Russia. The octagonal Belvedere, the park's most recent folly, dating from 1997, was inspired by the Palace of Pavlovsk in Saint Petersburg. It is decorated with large-scale ceramic designs based on paintings by Alexandre Serebriakoff, depicting the epic adventures of the Venetian Commedia dell'Arte puppets in their search for an ideal home. Perhaps they have found it here, facing the château with its gargoyles, and looking out over this "Jardin Remarquable" and the bucolic surrounding countryside. •

For visitors in search of nostalgia

♥ *Although the castle is not open to visitors, its stables have hosted "immersive tours" since 2024, taking visitors back to 1900. Traveling in a horse-drawn carriage or a vintage car, we set off to meet Eugène and Antoinette Schneider, owners of the château during the Belle Époque, and watch the preparations for their departure to Paris. On this journey through time, entitled* Le Grand Départ, *servants bustle about in impressive settings, ordering each other about noisily and enabling us—even the future-gazers among us—to forget the modern world for a moment.*

Practical Information

Parc Floral d'Apremont
32 Rue Madame-Eugène-Schneider
18150 Apremont-sur-Allier
Tel.: +33 (0)2 48 77 55 06
info@apremont-sur-allier.com

Opening Hours

➛ Late March–early October:
Open daily: 10:30 a.m.–12:30 p.m., 2 p.m.–6:30 p.m.

➛ Early October–early November:
Saturday and Sunday: 10:30 a.m.–12:30 p.m., 2 p.m.–6:30 p.m. (and every afternoon during the French fall break).

➛ Early November–late March:
Annual closure

➛ **apremont-sur-allier.com/en**

CHÂTEAU du LUDE

✲ Le Lude, Sarthe

Laid out beneath the walls of an imposing château, the gardens of Le Lude invite visitors to explore a maze, a rose garden, and an English-style landscape garden. Their terraces form an impressive spur of land, offering picturesque views over a rare traditional farming estate.

It was some forty years ago that Barbara, the young wife of the equally young Count de Nicolaÿ, left her native Flanders to move to her new home—and it was no ordinary home. The descendant of a dynasty stretching back to the feudal lords of the Middle Ages, the count was able to present her not only with her own charger but also with a château, one of the most prominent of the châteaux of the Loire.

It was from the bridge on the approach to the village of Le Lude that Barbara de Nicolaÿ caught her first glimpse of the imposing château emerging above the rooftops, its four façades flanked by six towers, and the whole ensemble presenting an illustrated history of French architecture over ten centuries. It made an impressive sight.

Spring was in full bloom and the birds were singing. An expert gardener, Barbara set about exploring the gardens, absorbed in the discoveries that awaited her. Their magnificent layout dated back to the seventeenth century, with a series of Italianate terraces stepping down to the Loir river running alongside the estate. But to her eye, they looked neglected. Surprised to see that none of the roses in the parterres and borders were in bloom, she quizzed the elderly head gardener about it. "That's because the Marquis de Talhouët only comes in the summer," was his reply. "I prune the roses in the middle of May, so they bloom in July, just in time for the marquis's arrival." It was an astonishing show of loyalty to a worthy ancestor who had passed away thirty years earlier.

The countess smiled, then took matters into her own hands. With the help of her brother, the landscape architect Augustin d'Ursel, she revived and restored the gardens, which are now classified as a "Jardin Remarquable." Then in 1994, she went further, establishing the yearly Fête des Jardiniers (Gardeners' Festival) and the Prix Pierre-Joseph Redouté, awarded annually to the best book on gardens and gardening published in French that year.

The château, built on an immense scale, looks out over the individually themed gardens and the magnificent panorama of the farmland opposite. Standing midway between Tours and Le Mans, it was originally a fortress occupied by the English during the Hundred Years' War. Then, in the fifteenth century, it came into the possession of Jehan de Daillon, chamberlain to Louis XI, and gradually the medieval castle was transformed into a pleasure palace on a monumental scale, standing 115 feet (35 meters) tall and covering an area of 25,500 square feet (2,000 square meters).

Each successive owner down the centuries has added a wing in the architectural style of the time, while taking care to preserve the traces of earlier buildings. Thus the mighty medieval round towers are surrounded by wings in Renaissance, neo-classical, and neo-Gothic style. One façade is embellished with sculpted medallions and mullion windows, while another features a broad pediment over a central building flanked by a pair of pavilions. In the main courtyard, meanwhile, the pilasters framing the windows are inlaid with black and pink marble. Each stone and every embellishment carries you off on a whirlwind journey through the centuries.

The château is open to the public, and its interior is as impressive as its exterior. One room is especially eye-catching: situated on the ground floor of the south-west tower, the studiolo, lined with paintings, is a feature that was frequently found in grand Italian residences, but is rare in French châteaux. The ceiling painting is by the School of Raphael, while the walls are painted with seven scenes ranging from *The Triumph of Chastity*, to a hunting scene, to *Noah's Ark*.

Outside, twenty acres (eight hectares) of elegant gardens are waiting to be discovered. On the top terrace, looking out over the valley, a stone balustrade stretching over 220 yards (200 meters) protects broderie parterres fringed with tulips, perennial geraniums, lavenders, salvias, and lilies. Waiting below, in the Jardin de l'Éperon (Spur Garden), is a maze of hornbeam, privet, and yew hedges. Should it disorientate you (as it is designed to do), you can regain your composure on the pretty benches positioned at the far end of the hedge-lined cul-de-sacs. Two more rooms enclosed by yew hedges complete this garden; one of them contains the rose garden, dedicated to Chinese roses, tea roses, and hybrid teas, with *Rosa chinensis* "Mutabilis" and the tea rose "Archiduc Joseph," among others, blooming from May to the first frosts—a graceful nod from the countess to the late marquis.

In the lower gardens, clipped yews and magnolias surround ponds whose still waters reflect a collection of sweet-scented shrubs. The very French design echoes in miniature the celebrated farmland on the opposite bank, which—in a leisurely way that seems almost incongruous to our eyes, since we are so used to seeing land exploited to the hilt—unfurls its meadows enclosed by copses of ancient trees to the horizon. The tranquil beauty of unadorned pastures grazed by Charolais cattle and horses induces the comforting feeling that the scene is impervious to the passage of time.

The gardens also boast a botanical walk featuring trees and shrubs from China, a legacy of the Chinese wife and the career of an eighteenth-century owner; an English landscape park that merges into the farming estate; and a kitchen garden. Laid out on three levels and over seven and a half acres (three hectares), its square compartments enclosed by box hedges contain heirloom tomatoes, eggplants, squash, fava beans, spinach, and a whole host of other vegetables. Surrounding them are apple, pear, peach, and apricot trees, and currant and raspberry bushes, filling the air with the sweet fragrance of their blossom in spring. Conservatories and an orangery complete this tour of the remarkable beauties of the gardens at Le Lude. •

Garden festival

♥ *The Fête des Jardiniers (Gardeners' Festival) is generally held in late May or early June, when dedicated gardeners and book lovers can share their questions and projects, and admire the plant collections of sixty or so exhibitors. A variety of workshops, with many aimed at children, are also available. On Sunday, visitors can learn how to make jam over a wood fire in the château's medieval kitchens, followed by a tasting of the results, spread over delicious crêpes.*

Practical Information

Château du Lude
4 Rue Jehan-de-Daillon
72800 Le Lude
Tel.: +33 (0)2 43 94 60 09
contact@lelude.com

Opening Hours

➛ April–September:
Open daily (including public holidays): around 10 a.m.–6 p.m. but opening hours vary, so check website before your visit or ring ahead.

➛ October:
Saturday and Sunday: 2 p.m.–6 p.m. (and every afternoon during the French fall break).

➛ December–early January:
Christmas break (apart from December 24, 25, 31, and January 1): 2 p.m.–6 p.m.

➛ Early January–end March:
Annual closure

➛ Check website for more details.

➛ Final admissions to the château 30 minutes before closing.

➛ **lelude.com/en**

Grand Est

Jardin de Berchigranges, Granges-sur-Vologne • Vosges

JARDIN de BERCHIGRANGES

✵ Granges-sur-Vologne, Vosges

Created with love, imagination, and determination, Berchigranges is an eclectic garden that nevertheless forms a coherent and exceptional ensemble. With its unique collection of daffodils, its spectacular displays of candelabra primulas, its moss garden, and its drifts of perennials in every shade of blue, it offers wonders at every turn.

When Thierry Dronet, a landscape gardener from the city, set out to make a garden from a plantation of spruce trees in an abandoned granite quarry in the Vosges, Monique, his future wife, greeted the idea with amused disbelief.

A plantswoman, plant collector, and native of this deeply rural region, she was initially dubious, but was soon won over by this incomer's exuberant imagination, unwavering determination, and delightfully hedonistic vision. The idea took root, and as love blossomed between the pair, so the new garden was born.

They brought in hundreds of truckloads of topsoil to improve the unpromising soil of the old quarry, uprooted hundreds of spruce trees, and waited: patience would be one of their most indispensable qualities in creating this seven-and-a-half-acre (three-hectare) enclosure at an altitude of 2,100 feet (650 meters).

Combining flights of fancy with a thoughtful and considered approach, the Dronets took the development of the garden one step at a time, allowing it to evolve over the years and through their changing ideas. Never drawing up any plans, they laid out the flower beds as they pulled up the spruce trees, concerned only about "recreating" nature as they went along and with restoring its luxuriance. And with their enviable gift for improvisation, they also invested much time in choosing the four thousand plant species from the northern hemisphere that now populate their little paradise, which has become a haven for a multitude of birds and insects.

The motto of these passionate gardeners is "Nature turns into a garden when people make it their pathway."

The motto of these passionate gardeners is "Nature turns into a garden when people make it their pathway." Over the years, they have created some twenty spaces with eclectic themes and atmospheres. Beds of old roses from the 1990s and a twenty-first-century meadow of wildflowers and grasses offer a beautiful illustration of the ways in which our relationship with nature has evolved over time.

As you stroll through the gardens or visit with the changing seasons, you are almost overwhelmed by a dizzying succession of choices. In the upper part of the garden you may decide to explore the Chambre des Dames (Ladies' Chamber): an intricately designed octagonal space enclosed by hornbeam hedges and devoted to scented plants, which forms an extension to the classic Jardin du Cottage (Cottage

Garden), with its charming mix of vegetables and perennials. But in a mischievous touch, the Dronets then suddenly lead you along smoothly cropped grassy paths into their Jardin du Flipper (Pinball Garden): a maze dominated by horizontal lines and the vertical shafts of yew trees. Thoroughly yet happily lost, you wander over little stone bridges accompanied by the sound of a rushing waterfall or babbling stream, before entering the felted silence of the moss garden. This Japanese-inspired exercise in chiaroscuro features more than two hundred local varieties of moss growing over large round stones, the vestiges of the old quarry. It is only at the end of this path with its almost ritualistic feeling, softened here by a bench and there by a pavilion for reading, that you reach the "dunes"—a meadow filled with native plants and airy perennials, apparently untouched by human hands.

The annual cycle of growth is constantly and gently punctuated by fleeting marvels as the seasons unfold. In April, Berchigranges celebrates the arrival of spring with more than three hundred and fifty varieties of daffodils and narcissi, amid gentle drifts of anemones, crocuses, muscari, and other bulbs. In May, visitors can wonder at the collection of candelabra primulas in every shade, accompanied by geraniums, violas, and alpine flowers including the heavenly blue of gentians. June is a sea of blue, with sumptuous Himalayan poppies, campanulas, delphiniums, and the vivid blue spires of anchusas. July is the time for roses, while August sees an explosion of phlox and eryngium, cirsium and angelica, cimicifuga, eupatorium, and a host of other giants, vying with each other with their colors and fragrances. In September, grasses are backlit by the low sun and the emphasis is on shape and movement. October is perhaps the most romantic and tranquil of all, with its lacy filigrees of foliage and seedheads in shades of bronze and silver.

The annual cycle of growth is constantly and gently punctuated by fleeting marvels as the seasons unfold.

Generational, seasonal, and resolutely modern, this gently rolling walk transports the visitor to lovingly tended universes that are constantly enriched by their creators. As Monique Dronet reminds us, "You don't always have to look for flowers, you just need to look, smell, and listen. Nature is here, whatever the season, magnificent and captivating." •

Sunsets and birch sap

♥ *Visitors can now rent the Plantes et Plumes chalet, set in the heart of the garden: a 1,300-square-foot (120-square-meter) oasis offering comfort and elegant surroundings reflecting the taste of its owners, with a 320-square-foot (30-square-meter) terrace overlooking the meadow. Guests also have access to the garden from sunrise to sunset, in all seasons. To complete this nature retreat, birch sap—a traditional detox and folk remedy reputed to offer many health benefits—is available to buy on site or at the Ferme des Bouleaux Blancs next door.*

Practical Information

Jardin de Berchigranges
9 Berchigranges
88640 Granges-sur-Vologne
Tel.: +33 (0)3 29 51 47 19

Opening Hours

➛ April–May and September:
Wednesday–Sunday and public holidays:
2 p.m.–6 p.m.

➛ June–August:
Wednesday–Sunday and public holidays:
10 a.m.–6 p.m.

➛ October–end March:
Annual closure

➛ Pets, picnics, and toy vehicles are not permitted on site.

➛ **berchigranges.com**

Hauts-de-France

Jardin du Mont des Récollets, Cassel • Nord
Jardins de Séricourt, Séricourt • Pas-de-Calais
Abbaye de Valloires, Argoules • Somme

JARDIN du Mont des RÉCOLLETS

✲ Cassel,
Nord

This Flemish garden is the very image of those created and painted here in the Renaissance period. Set amid an unspoiled landscape, it combines a passion for topiary with a contemporary desire to create a setting where visitors feel at ease.

"In the North," as an old French saying goes, "we cry twice: once when we arrive, and once when we leave." And yet the welcoming landscapes of Houtland, in the heart of French Flanders, are gentle and rolling, dotted with farmhouses featuring stepped gables and painted shutters, hop gardens, and traditional small cafés or *estaminets*. And they are home to talented landscape gardeners who are passionate about their culture and their roots.

Escaping from a world that was "too globalized," Emmanuel de Quillacq settled on the slopes of Le Mont des Récollets, halfway between Lille and Dunkirk, in the 1980s. Heir to a family farm dating from the seventeenth century and a graduate of the École Nationale Supérieure de Paysage, he began his career as a landscape gardener by . . . filling wheelbarrows with rubble.

The L-shaped farm building, with a typically Flemish pantile roof, was at that time in a dilapidated state. The garden consisted of a walnut tree, a handful of willows, and a great deal of rubble, and the student was short of funds. So de Quillacq took his time, while never forgetting where his final ambitions lay. Armed with his agricultural, horticultural, and landscaping skills, he embarked on lengthy research into his Flemish heritage, and, step by step, he created a veritable Flemish Garden of Eden.

"In the North," as an old French saying goes, "we cry twice: once when we arrive, and once when we leave."

From its origins in the medieval period, the Flemish garden reached its heyday during the Renaissance, gaining immortality in the paintings of Rubens, Van Eyck, and Brueghel. Slightly overshadowed by formal gardens *à la française*, it sometimes overlapped with them in its geometrical rigor. Although the Flemish garden had several variations, they all shared the same characteristics: they were small in scale and were distinctive for their symmetrical structure made up of multiple hedges and topiary, their use of brick and blue stone, their screens, their lack of relief, and, invariably, their water features.

Another charming aspect of the gardens around Flemish farmhouses, which has been explored and enhanced at Le Mont des Récollets, is the way in which the design gradually grows more relaxed: highly sophisticated around the building itself, the design becomes less and less formal as you progress deeper into the outdoors, until at the invisible boundary with the surrounding wooded countryside it shades into an apparently natural planting of perennials and grasses.

Laid out over just under four acres (one and a half hectares), Emmanuel de Quillacq's garden—also known as "Wouwenberg"—consists of twenty-two small green rooms designed as an extension of the house, with hedges forming the walls and corridors of the themed rooms in chiaroscuro.

In the first room—the Chambre sur Cour (Courtyard Room)—immaculately clipped yew topiary lines the wall of the brick farmhouse, the flat tops of the yews making an elegant nod to the stepped gable of the façade. In the front, the clipped yews combine with a row of white hydrangeas to form a grassy avenue leading to the next rooms.

The Chambre des Berlingots (Berlingot Room), as sober as it is baroque, is emblematic of the garden. Renamed the "Antwerp Diamond Garden" by the landscape architect's Belgian friends, it is crisscrossed with box clipped into tetrahedrons, like the candy it is named for, resembling the Flanders countryside viewed from the sky, with fields separated by hedges forming a vast checkerboard pattern.

Another chessboard—this time almost black and white—makes up the Chambre du Nord (North Room). Here, the box borders form low squares and enclose plants with black, white, or green foliage, such as ophiopogon and leptinella. Next to this room is the Chambre du Printemps (Spring Room), with severe outlines that are softened by beds of brilliant blue and mauve hydrangeas.

The legacy of the Flemish masters can be seen both inside and outside the garden; as a skilled landscape designer, Emmanuel de Quillacq has taken care to integrate these external spaces into the site. Unlike some of his fellow designers who are keen to cut down trees to create a "clear view," he prefers to lop and top to form a succession of frames that focus the gaze on the surrounding woods and fields, the pale sky, and the colorful farm buildings. In the same spirit, round windows cut into the hedges open up unexpected vistas, revealing the beauty within the beauty, leaving you wondering whether the final composition is formed by the landscape or the garden.

Along with the Chambre Bleue (Blue Room)—a tribute to the Renaissance—these three large checkerboards thus structure the garden within its setting of willow and oak trees. In spring and summer, the spaces within them are filled with hundreds of thousands of bulbs, including crocuses, tulips, and muscari. Roses, gladioli, and alliums bloom as the seasons unfold, merging into a sea of perennials, mostly in shades of blue.

This ornamental garden also contains a large orchard, a kitchen garden, and a rose garden, remaining faithful to images in sixteenth- and seventeenth-century history and art history, in which apples are forever the forbidden fruit and roses the flowers of paradise.

Since its creation and its opening to the public, the Jardin du Mont des Récollets has been named "Garden of the Year 2011" by the French Association of Garden and Horticulture Journalists. It was also voted "France's favorite garden" in 2013, on the television show of the same name, presented by Stéphane Bern, and it has been awarded the accolade of "Jardin Remarquable." ♣

Refreshments in the garden

Located in a wing of the farmhouse, the garden's café features circular wooden tables, paneled walls, garlands of lights and pumpkins, old paintings and candlesticks, and a delectable view of the gardens, providing visitors with the ideal spot to enjoy lunch or a drink. From spring onwards, it also offers a terrace among the topiary and flowers. An occasional small flea market completes the authentic Flemish character of this estaminet.

Practical Information

Jardin du Mont des Récollets
1936 Route de Steenvoorde
59670 Cassel
Tel.: +33 (0)6 07 84 77 50
jardindumontdesrecollets@gmail.com

Opening Hours

- Late March–late September:
Thursday–Sunday: 10 a.m.–6 p.m.

- Late September–late March:
Annual closure

- Self-guided tours, and guided group tours available by appointment.

- **parcsetjardins.fr/jardins/626-jardin-du-mont-des-recollets** (in French)

JARDINS de SÉRICOURT

Séricourt,
Pas-de-Calais

In an area of northern France that has been riven with conflict in past centuries, two generations of the Gosse de Gorre family have created a moving commemoration in the form of this tranquil retreat.

There are many ways to sweep away the memory of soldiers and civilians who died in wars. But there are also many ways to honor their memory, resolutely and in the name of humanity. And perhaps the most tender and graceful way of all is by creating a garden for them.

At Séricourt, the Gosse de Gorre family—two generations of landscape gardeners—share their lives and tend their garden together, while respecting and remaining faithful to the spirit of their land. Their refined and constantly evolving project stands as a moving, poetic, and thought-provoking testimony to their skills and their vision.

Yves Gosse de Gorre, a graduate of the École Supérieure du Jardin et du Paysage in Anderlecht, Belgium, acquired this eleven-acre (four-and-a-half-hectare) plot of land between Le Touquet and Arras, about sixty miles (one hundred kilometers) from Dieppe, in the early 1980s. A grower and lover of hardy perennials, he started out as a nurseryman with a few displays in front of his house. But the landscape gardener in him began to grow impatient, and he decided to try his hand at his first garden. Once the hardest part—getting started—was behind him, Gosse de Gorre wholeheartedly threw himself into the project and carried on creating more and more green rooms; thirty years on, the gardens at Séricourt are made up of thirty or so of these rooms. Meanwhile, Yves's son Guillaume, who completed his studies at the École Nationale Supérieure de Paysage in Versailles, had joined him, and since 2017 Guillaume has become the "guardian and custodian of the spirit of the gardens."

The site of the gardens and the neighboring plateau were devastated by the Hundred Years' War and many later conflicts, culminating in the destruction of a world war that defied all understanding. The vestiges of World War I trenches and shell holes can still be seen in the surrounding area. For the two gardeners, it was clear that they had to find a way of symbolizing these permanent scars on the landscape.

They therefore created gardens dedicated to war and peace. In the first of these, two armies, represented by Irish yews trimmed into spindle shapes, confront each other in imposing numbers across a broad grassy avenue. Further on, giant warrior "masks" in clipped box loom in a menacing green mass, with grimacing expressions beneath beetling eyebrows. Beyond those lies the devastation of the battlefield, embodied by drifts of corn poppies that turn the meadow scarlet—a reference to the poppies that clothed the churned-up fields and bomb craters after World War I, and which, for the British, became an enduring symbol of the sacrifice of war.

Happily, peace is glimpsed at last, with the vista of a giant cross in clipped box and a path lined with creeping willow with silky blue-green foliage, the mauve spires of

perovskia, and pink “Rush” and “Ballerina” roses, their soft pastel palette offering a soothing invitation to negotiations.

This is the antechamber to the glorious arches of the Cathédrale des Roses (Cathedral of Roses), an iconic feature of the garden that invites many interpretations. Created by Yves Gosse de Gorre to celebrate the new millennium in the year 2000, it is also a tribute to the cathedral builders of the first millennium, a celebration of peace restored, and a nod to himself as the master builder of a cathedral of plants.

Along its seventy-yard (sixty-four meter) length, metallic arches are clad in roses, wisteria, and crimson glory vine. Varieties of clematis clamber up pleached trees, and “side chapels” spill over with old roses. Beneath this profusion of vigorous climbing and rambling roses, including white “Seagull” and deep pink “American Pillar,” visitors stroll along the velvety lawn and down the meandering paths as though in a dream.

Peace also reigns in the Jardin des Topiaires (Topiary Garden), where box blight—every gardener’s nightmare—led to the removal of much of the box. The topiaries, in every shape and size, from the classically formal to the wildly fanciful, have been diversified to include clipped azaleas and heathers alongside the box and hornbeam.

As well as symbolizing wisdom and folly, war and peace, and displaying French and English influences, the gardens at Séricourt are also a laboratory of experimental botanical ideas for their creators. An example of this is the Clos des Roses Keiji (Keiji Rose Garden) created by Guillaume Gosse de Gorre—the fruit of a year-long Franco-Japanese collaboration with the rose breeder Rose Farm Keiji in the Kyoto region. These hybrid roses are unique in France.

There is also the Chambre Jaune (Yellow Room), which plays on every shade of this sunny color through its roses, rudbeckia, and hedges of forsythia, glowing gold in spring; and, in a modern twist, the grass maze, a fleeting forerunner of the wild-flower meadows so beloved of contemporary gardeners, featuring graceful miscanthus and pennisetum swaying in the breeze among brightly colored echinaceas.

Always inventive and often unique, the many green rooms offer a comprehensive tour of the art of planting. A pond and water garden planted with water lilies, horsetails, and water iris provide biodiversity. A Chambre Grise (Gray Room) leads us to the end—or perhaps to the beginning—with its "caged" shrubs and parterres, enclosed by somber gravel paths. But there is also water, at first barely visible as a little rill between the flower beds, then swelling into a fountain at the foot of the garden. Here, a white sculpture of a human figure by Robert Arnoux raises cupped hands up towards the stream of clear water. In a dark and troubled world, it seems to say, humankind can embody hope if we return to what is essential. •

And there's more

Don't miss the Rendez-Vous aux Jardins on the first weekend of June, which offers a behind-the-scenes glimpse of this remarkable garden. Visitors can learn more about its powerful symbolism through guided tours with the Séricourt gardeners scheduled throughout the weekend. All questions are welcome, and no booking is required.

Practical Information

Jardins de Séricourt
2 Rue du Bois
62270 Séricourt
Tel.: +33 (0)3 21 03 64 42
lgdeg@jardindesericourt

Opening Hours

➻ May–August:
Tuesday–Saturday: 10 a.m.–7 p.m.
Sunday and public holidays: 3 p.m.–7 p.m.

➻ September–October:
Thursday–Saturday: 10 a.m.–7 p.m.
Sunday and public holidays: 3 p.m.–7 p.m.

➻ November–end April:
Annual closure

➻ Final admissions one hour before closing.

➻ Free parking available on site. Small, leashed dogs are permitted on weekdays only.

➻ **jardindesericourt.com** (in French)

ABBAYE de VALLOIRES

✵ Argoules, Somme

Created by the renowned landscape designer Gilles Clément, the gardens of the Abbaye de Valloires offer an eclectic combination of arboretum islands, a large rose garden, and even a tribute to the eighteenth-century naturalist Jean-Baptiste de Lamarck and his classification of clouds. A visit to these abbey gardens is a chance to marvel and learn.

To listen to Gilles Clément, you might think that the profession of landscape gardener requires a degree of humility that is not granted to everybody. When an architect contemplates their work, it generally corresponds to their initial plans. With a garden, it is a completely different matter. The landscape architect is the director, choreographing the different elements, but is never in control. On the contrary, nature is in charge, leaving gardeners free to indulge their artistic freedom.

For nature and gardeners alike, the garden is both a stage and untamed territory; seeds spread themselves at will, artists in box topiary invent new forms, a bed of red roses spills over on to its more ethereal neighbors, a gust of wind carries off the leaves of a plain green shrub and deposits them on an island bed of kaleidoscopic colors.

In the end, which is never really the end, with the passing of the hours, seasons, and years, the garden no longer bears much resemblance to the design. And in truth it never is the same, because it is a living thing; and this is precisely what Gilles Clément, a tireless observer of his own landscape gardens, loves so much about it.

This great theorist of the contemporary garden has distilled his numerous experiences into concepts. His "gardens in motion" and "planetary gardens" advocate, above all, the freedom and harmony of the living world: a delightful paradox when you devote your talents and your existence to the ordering and shaping of nature. The results range from the Mediterranean luxuriance of the Domaine du Rayol in the Var to the urban sophistication of the Parc André-Citroën in Paris. The earliest of these creations was the garden at the Abbaye de Valloires, which he designed in 1987.

When Gilles Clément first visited the site, which consisted of fields and meadows stretching out beneath the walls of the immense Cistercian abbey in the valley of the Authie river, a few miles from the Bay of the Somme, he noted that the *parvis* was too short and the land was long and sloping. He drew up a plan with a long perspective stretching towards the horizon, a kind of "architectural silence" to echo the austerity and symmetry of the eighteenth-century façade.

It was in this elongated space that he laid out his gardens, extending them over the rolling landscape crisscrossed by streams. Like an artist composing a painting, he created five gardens over twenty acres (eight hectares), incorporating styles that ranged from geometric to flamboyant, from sublimely classical to scholarly modernist, from the formal garden *à la française* to the romantic English garden.

Working with Jean-Louis Cousin, a nurseryman from Pas-de-Calais with a significant plant collection, Clément planted five thousand plant varieties in the spaces he had designed for them. Many of these originated from Asia and America, and Cousin made it his mission to acclimatize them to the soil and climate of Picardy.

The Cistercian abbey of Valloires housed up to four hundred monks in its heyday. The cloister, enclosed by its four arcaded passages, was its central feature. Still standing today, it now houses a small French garden. A stroll through it may well be accompanied by the murmurs of prayers that have been chanted there for six centuries. This is a spot to meditate on time.

At the other end of the garden, a cloister of plants contrasts with its stone counterpart. Yew and hornbeam trees clipped into pillars punctuate beds of lavender and old roses, while a 250-year-old pear tree—one of the oldest in France and a living witness to the passage of time and monastic life—embellishes the abbey façade and twines around its windows. The Cistercian monks would use its fruit to make a liqueur that they exported as far as the kingdom of England. The monks who lived in these places of religious devotion would spend their days not only in study and prayer, but also cultivating the land.

In front of the abbey, on the site of the former kitchen garden, is a magnificent rose garden. Covering over half an acre (a quarter hectare), it contains eighty varieties

of rose, including the glorious clear pink Rosa "Jardins de Valloires," along with the bright red David Austin English rose "Picardy," scarlet "La Sevillana," pure white "Summer Snow," and pale pink "Bonica." Together they form an intoxicating rose garden, with much to admire, learn from, and simply revel in.

The abbey church burned down and was rebuilt in the eighteenth century. At a time when it was being deserted by some of its flock, the mighty Roman Catholic Church decided to rebuild on a grand scale: medieval asceticism was abandoned in favor of the rococo and the baroque. Woodwork, paintings, sculptures, gilding, and decorative details were all designed to impress parishioners and bring them back into the fold. While the resulting number of penitents and converts remains unconfirmed, one thing is certain: the new church was beautiful. The monumental organ, in particular, is magnificent both to look at and to listen to; unlike many church organs, the upper part, case, and balustrades form a single carved wooden ensemble, with rich, clear acoustics that are the envy of organists from all over France.

Spending a few moments immersed in sacred music before setting off to explore a garden dedicated to the eighteenth-century naturalist Jean-Baptiste Lamarck makes for a remarkable juxtaposition. Here, the straight avenues are replaced by wooden steps representing the stages of the evolution of plants, with very ancient plants, such as ferns, ginkgos, and horsetails, leading up to much more youthful grasses.

In the Jardin des Îles (Island Garden), imagination is equaled only by the freshness of the concept. Here, plants are grouped not by species but by color and shape. Arranged in islands of silver, gold, or lilac, they form a romantic English landscape within these gardens that have earned the prestigious "Jardin Remarquable" label. •

Painting Valloires

These islands of color are the perfect embodiment of the Valloires gardens: a haven of vibrant beauty and isolated serenity surrounded by farmland. And speaking of color, the Journée des Peintres (Painters' Day) is a new annual event that takes place at the abbey in June. Beginner, amateur, and experienced painters are invited to a workshop on the abbey's spacious lawns to try their hand at watercolor painting or "poetic infusion," and to sip a cocktail at the end of the day while enjoying everyone's work.

Practical Information

Abbaye de Valloires
80120 Argoules
Tel.: +33 (0)3 22 23 53 55

Opening Hours

- Late March–April:
  Open daily: 10 a.m.–6 p.m.
- May–August:
  Open daily: 10 a.m.–7 p.m.
- September:
  Open daily: 10 a.m.–6:30 p.m.
- October–early November:
  Open daily: 10 a.m.–5:30 p.m.
- Early November–late March:
  Annual closure
- Final admissions one hour before closing.
- **jardinsdevalloires.fr**

Normandy

Jardin Botanique de Vauville, Vauville • Manche
Jardin Plume, Auzouville-sur-Ry • Seine-Maritime
Jardins du Château de Brécy, Creully-sur-Seulles • Calvados
Jardins du Montperthuis, Chemilli • Orne
Jardin Jungle Karlostachys, Eu • Seine-Maritime
Bois des Moutiers, Varengeville-sur-Mer • Seine-Maritime

JARDIN Botanique de VAUVILLE

✲ Vauville, Manche

Tended by three successive generations of gardener-botanists, the botanical garden at Vauville is also aptly known as the "traveler's garden." Looking out over the sea to distant horizons, it offers a tour of the world's beauties, paying tribute to the richness of plant life around the globe.

The botanical garden at Vauville is a relatively youthful creation, born out of the ruins and hopes of the years after World War II. Its creator, Éric Pellerin—a sailor from the age of twenty, who became a chemical engineer in the perfume industry—was a lover of travel, life, and fragrances. It was in the 1930s that this globetrotter and admirer of the botanists and gardeners of the southern hemisphere discovered La Hague: a shimmering expanse of moorland and heath, dominated by a castle complete with keep, on the far north-western tip of the Cotentin peninsula. The die was cast. Enchanted by this wild bay battered by the winds and enveloped by sea mists, Éric Pellerin metamorphosed into an armchair traveler, though without shedding any of his adventurous spirit—a delightful paradox that lies at the origins of this "traveler's garden."

The botanical garden at Vauville is a journey within a journey.

His capacity for backbreaking work was matched only by his imagination, boldness, and passion. At that time, the Château de Vauville, formerly the stronghold of the Haubert dynasty, was surrounded by pastureland stretching to the sea—a twenty-acre (eight-hectare) carpet of lush grass, grazed by cattle and horses.

And so it was that in 1947, Éric Pellerin and his wife Nicole not only embarked on the rebuilding of the great house after years of wartime damage, but also embraced the challenge of transforming this grazing land into a haven devoted exclusively to evergreen plants from the southern hemisphere. Piercing an archway through the castle's curtain wall, they took advantage of the shelter provided by the former moat to plant their first Tasmanian tree ferns and Monterey cypresses.

Protected by the warm waters of the Gulf Stream, plants and trees from distant climes found a microclimate on this deserted headland that resembled their native environment. This remarkable plant collection is unique in Normandy; conceived, nurtured, designed, and enlarged by three generations of Pellerins, all of whom have shared a passion for botany and travel, it now covers twelve acres (five hectares).

It was a bold venture, for the mildness of the Gulf Stream is not always enough to mitigate the harshness of the salt-laden westerly winds. The castle's curtain wall provides some protection, and evergreen trees and shrubs chosen for their hardiness have been planted in dense hedges to shield the more delicate plants.

Laid out as a series of green rooms and enlivened by a sequence of ponds, the garden contains more than nine hundred plant species from the southern hemisphere, with the addition over the years of oleanders, agaves, and palm trees from the shores of the Mediterranean. Nearly seven hundred feet (two hundred meters) above the buffeting waves of the English Channel, visitors can stroll among Chilean fire bushes, bamboos, ginkgos, fuchsia-flowered grevilleas (spider flowers) from Australia, magnolias, and jasmine, its fragrant white flowers twining around the palm trees.

This eco-friendly tropical paradise, embellished with stone features of Indian and Asian inspiration, has been classified as a "Jardin Remarquable" since 2004. The stream that used to flow through the fields now feeds the various ponds, where aquatic plants flourish in the shade of huge emerald-green royal ferns and tree peonies with their enormous pink blooms.

As Éric Pellerin—the current owner and as dynamic a character as his grandfather—says, this botanical garden is a journey within a journey. From Cherbourg, you cross fourteen miles (twenty-three kilometers) of the rugged and unspoiled Cotentin peninsula to find yourself suddenly entering a different hemisphere, for a stroll through this flamboyant oasis. •

Sleep or dine at the château

All that remains of the feudal fortress today are the keep, the circular curtain wall, and the moat. Two wings, rebuilt and enlarged in the original style in the seventeenth and nineteenth centuries, form a right angle around the keep. Romantic but rugged, the Château de Vauville is characteristic of the northern Cotentin, and its façade and shale roofs were listed as historic monuments in 1972. Notable inhabitants down the centuries have included Thomas of Biville, chaplain to Louis IX (Saint Louis), and Napoleon's aide-de-camp, General Le Marois, who had bees—the imperial cipher—painted on the dining room ceiling.

Renovated some thirty years ago by the Pellerin family, the handsome château with its stained-glass windows is not open to visitors. A dedicated wing, however, provides accommodation for one or more nights, in elegant guest rooms with evocative names such as the Chambre du Poète (Poet's Chamber), Chambre du Voyageur (Traveler's Chamber), and Chambre du Peintre (Painter's Chamber). Groups can also book lunch or dinner here and enjoy the spacious lounge and private garden for a few hours.

The Vauville farm

After the flora comes the fauna. Following in the inventive footsteps of Éric Pellerin, his grandson—also Éric—and Guillaume de Lestrange have created the Vauville farm as a conservatory of Anglo-Norman breeds, some of which are endangered. Guided tours of the garden and farm, followed by workshops on geography, scents, and drawing, are available for school groups. Families can also enjoy the educational trail leading from the Blanc de Hotot rabbit to the Bayeux pig, via the Crèvecoeur chicken, the Rouen duck, and, of course, the Normande cow. From tropical vegetation to local menagerie, this extraordinary garden unites them all.

Practical Information

Jardin Botanique de Vauville
1 Route du Thôt
50440 La Hague
Tel.: +33 (0)2 33 10 00 00
info@jardin-vauville.fr

Opening Hours

➻ Late March–September:
Monday: 12 p.m.–7 p.m. (until 8 p.m. in July and August).
Tuesday–Sunday: 2 p.m.–7 p.m. (until 8 p.m. in July and August).

➻ October (weather permitting):
Wednesday–Sunday (open daily during the French fall break): 2 p.m.–6 p.m.

➻ November–late March:
Annual closure

➻ Open all day for group tours (reservation required, minimum fifteen people, on-site catering available).

➻ **jardin-vauville.fr**

JARDIN PLUME

Auzouville-sur-Ry, Seine-Maritime

Described by a British garden writer as the "most beautiful contemporary garden in France," the Jardin Plume is an inspiring lesson in mass planting of feathery grasses. Its baroque hedges contain breathtaking compositions of tall perennials that offer a flamboyant display in the fall.

There are no classic flower beds or billowing mounds of pink hydrangeas at Jardin Plume. Here, the grass grows untamed and unabashed, and delicate, feathery plants mingle and sway in the breeze in voluptuous waves. This apparently artless "wilderness," which changes palette with the seasons, is in fact the product of over twenty years of work and of unflagging creative flair.

In the beginning there was an orchard, where red eating apples were harvested by the bucketful. When landscape gardeners Patrick and Sylvie Quibel arrived here in 1997, they had a vision that—with all due respect to the traditional products of Normandy—aspired to something more ambitious than cider and *compôte de pommes*. Before them lay a flat, grassy expanse of seven and a half acres (three hectares), open to the south. All around, farmland stretched to the surrounding woodland. Seventeen miles (twenty-seven kilometers) from Rouen, in the Seine-Maritime département, these soft meadows, virtually untouched by pruning shears, seemed to be waiting for their full potential to be revealed.

Hugely inspired by English, Italian, and Dutch gardens, the Quibels are leading members of the contemporary trend towards naturalistic planting and the

New Perennial Movement, pioneered by the inventive Dutch nurseryman and landscape designer Piet Oudolf. Concentrating on herbaceous perennials and grasses, they set out to recreate the feeling of spontaneous and exuberant natural growth.

But for this endeavor, certain conditions are required, needless to say, and here history and culture play their part. Patrick and Sylvie Quibel had also inherited gardens that were laid out in the seventeenth-century baroque style. The native plants, fine agrostis (bentgrass), fragrant flouve or sweet vernal grass, and lofty American veronicastrum that they planted together and encouraged to mingle freely therefore formed a striking contrast with the grid structure of their clipped box or hornbeam squares that contained them.

Over the years, the topiary has been clipped with virtuoso skill by Sébastien Damiens, the head gardener, whose most stunning tour de force is the long and undulating box hedge that he has shaped by eye to echo the waving of the plants.

This meticulously designed garden, awarded the "Jardin Remarquable" label, is divided into five spaces that explore the nuances and moods of the passing seasons.

In the Jardin d'Automne (Autumn Garden), the Quibels set out to allay the pangs of nostalgia that accompany the end of summer with the loveliest of late-flowering plants. The tall white candlesticks of cimicifuga, purple and white American vernonias, and small-flowered mauve asters are only some of the delicate, airy perennials that spill out of their beds and brush against us as we walk along the narrow paths. Engulfed by tall, waving grasses, we are transported back to childhood, and the wistful melancholy of the season is momentarily lifted.

These "gardens within a garden" are laid out around the long apple orchard, which remains the central feature, with its immaculately mowed paths and lawns framing squares brimming with grasses, bulbs, and native wildflowers. Yellow rattle helps to reduce the fertility of the soil to allow the native plants to flourish, and the squares are cut once a year in mid-October.

For the Jardin d'Été (Summer Garden), leveled into a platform to the south of the old brick and timber farmhouse, the Quibels chose a warm palette of red, gold, orange, and yellow, with "Eole" dahlias, scarlet with yellow centers, tall annual sunflowers, crocosmias, hemerocallis, rudbeckias, poppies, and sprawling nasturtiums, among grasses selected to add yet more color. In full bloom in high summer it is a riot of color against the open squares of immaculately clipped box.

The Jardin Plume (Feather Garden)—the first space to be planted and the one that inspired the others and gave the whole garden its name—is an ethereal, impressionistic composition of tall, airy plants, dancing in the breeze and viewed against the light. Here there is no large foliage, no bold flowers, but instead, in the designers' words, "fine spikes, mists, and cascades of tiny flowers," with tall veronicastrum and thalictrum, *Phlox paniculata* and aquilegias among the feathery plumes of grasses, the rhythm of their planting and movement echoed by the undulating architecture of the long wavy box hedge.

Finally, the Jardin des Fleurs (Flower Garden), surrounded by a picket fence, occupies the site of the former kitchen garden, which has been enlarged while preserving its original structure. Annuals, biennials, and perennials have been chosen to merge naturally and to bloom for six months of the year, without recourse to traditional bedding plants. Drifts of zinnias and lupins, poppies and love-in-a-mist, tobacco plants and *Asperula orientalis*, take over gradually from each other, punctuated by tall mulleins and feathery fennel and dill. Clipped box provides the architectural structure for changing compositions that showcase the apparently spontaneous abundance that is the hallmark of the garden. •

The nursery and orchard

One of the joys here is the nursery, where visitors can buy many of the plants they have admired. From the terrace or promontory they can also enjoy a panorama over the gardens, highlighting their variety, their flawless geometry, and their breathtaking views of the Normandy countryside. And from a cart shed converted into a summer living room, they can relish the translucency of slender grasses and misty cascades of flowers against the light. In the orchard, meanwhile, wooden deckchairs surround a mirror-like pool reflecting the blues and grays of the sky, inviting a moment's pause to rest and contemplate.

Practical Information

Jardin Plume
790 Rue de la Plaine
76116 Auzouville-sur-Ry
Tel.: +33 (0)2 35 23 00 01
lejardinplume@gmail.com

Opening Hours

(Garden and nursery)

➛ May–mid-October:
Wednesday: 10 a.m.–12 p.m., 2 p.m.–6 p.m.
Thursday and Friday: 2 p.m.–6 p.m.
Saturday: 10 a.m.–12 p.m., 2 p.m.–6 p.m.
Sunday: 2 p.m.–6 p.m.

➛ Mid-October–end April:
Annual closure

➛ May 1, May 8, and August 15: 2 p.m.–6 p.m.

➛ Pentecost Monday and July 14: closed

➛ Plumes d'Été festival held last weekend of June: 10 a.m.–6 p.m.

➛ **lejardinplume.com**

JARDINS du Château de BRÉCY

✵ Creully-sur-Seulles, Calvados

A jewel of Italian Renaissance garden design, the gardens of the Château de Brécy feature precisely carved stonework, immaculately clipped greenery, and terraces offering long vistas that draw the eye up to the heavens.

The immense length of the perspective here is reminiscent of the gardens of Versailles or the châteaux of the Loire, although curiously the château lies at the foot of the gardens, which seem to climb upwards to infinity. It is an unusual and disconcerting architectural arrangement that challenges our sense of geography. Where are we? Is this Vaux-le-Vicomte, or perhaps Chambord? A clue to the more northerly position lies in the former description of the château as a "*demeure manable*," a term used exclusively in Normandy to distinguish bourgeois residences from barns and stables. A journalist writing in the daily newspaper *L'Éclair* in 1903 described Brécy as a "little Versailles lost in the fields."

In this unexpected setting deep in the countryside between Bayeux and Caen stands the seventeenth-century Château de Brécy, home to one of the few Renaissance gardens in France, and the only one in the Calvados region to have retained its original layout.

A journalist writing in the daily newspaper* L'Éclair *in 1903 described Brécy as "a little Versailles lost in the fields."

The Benedictine priory that once stood on the site was abandoned during the Wars of Religion, and the next owner of the estate built the house with its slate roof. In 1638, Jacques Le Bas, president of the court of Caen, bought the estate and added outbuildings on either side of the main dwelling to give the ensemble its U-shape. He added dormer windows in the roof and topped the whole with a turret, before embarking on the layout of the gardens. In this endeavor he was aided by his son, a canon at Bayeux Cathedral who had made many journeys to Rome.

It is to this cleric that Brécy owes the terraced design that was such a distinguishing feature of Italian Renaissance architecture. There are four terraces, increasing in width to enhance the perspective and covering some two and a half acres (more than a hectare), culminating in imposing wrought-iron gates opening onto the hillside and the sky. According to Didier Wirth, the current owner, this plan was inspired by a bereavement. The canon's sister Estelle had died young and was buried in the church beside the house, and the gardens were designed to embody the earthly paradise, leading through these ornate gates to the heavens.

In the twentieth century, Brécy fell into neglect, like so many other great estates, and was only rescued when a couple who combined passion with perseverance arrived: Didier and Barbara Wirth. Didier Wirth was president of the Comité des Parcs et Jardins de France for twenty years, and his wife Barbara was an accomplished gardener and sculptor. When they embarked on the restoration of the estate in the 1990s it was not before time: "Water was coming out of the walls, and the steps were

crumbling." It took four years of building and drainage work before they could embark on a meticulous reconstruction of the planting to complement the imposing stone structure.

In the 1950s, their predecessor, the writer Jacques de Lacretelle, had planted the intricate broderie parterres on the lowest terrace, faithfully reproducing the parterres designed by Henri IV's gardener. In a tribute to Brécy's monastic past, a hornbeam cloister leads to the terrace with two large pools. The garden was completely enclosed by walls and had no water, so the Wirths added these water features, each with a central stone fountain sculpted by Barbara—one in the form of a wicker basket and the other a mound of artichokes. This terrace, enlivened by the sound of water, is set within another larger one, with paths and avenues that invite visitors to stroll.

Eleven flights of stone steps climb up the hill, punctuated by acanthus leaf balustrades, heraldic lions, elegant sculptures, and pilasters. Jacques Le Bas and his son calculated the alignment of the spaces with precision. From their first-floor windows, the Wirths could take in at a glance the rising terraces, which have been

elegantly recreated. Lining the central path are long clipped box hedges, topiary trees, ribbons of hornbeam, holly balls in Versailles planters, and tapering yew cones, their many delicate shades of green creating a flawless symmetry and grace.

From the lowest terrace to the very top, it is as though you are traveling through time, step by step, through medieval and Italian influences to reach the rigorously geometrical synthesis of the French formal garden. Before the gateway to the heavens you reach a first gateway, as if in preparation for the ascent—both symbolically and literally—of the grassy hillside, under the ever-changing Normandy sky.

Outside the walls, beech trees shield the gardens from the north winds, while on the south side, smaller trees allow the sun to shine through. The ploughed fields that used to surround the hill, meanwhile, have been transformed into orchards.

This canopy of trees in the heart of the bocage offer protection to the terraces, so that they can display their shades of green and their majestic architecture in all seasons, while plantings of blue and white flowers, carefully chosen by Barbara Wirth, soften their geometric severity.

Tulips, irises, peonies, alliums, and magnolias are scattered throughout the gardens. A collection of laurels, white-flowered osmanthus, and hollies embellish the last terrace, while white roses glow against the pale stone of the château façades and clematis and agapanthus vie with each other in their shades of blue and mauve. Behind the church, old roses fill the air with their fragrance.

A monumental Ionic gateway stands at the entrance to the estate, an imposing prelude to this contemplative journey through time. The gateway and terraces are listed as a historic monument, while the garden has been awarded the label of "Jardin Remarquable."

For Didier Wirth, what matters most is that a garden should reflect the spirit of place. This alliance between nature and stone may waver, but when it proves fruitful, or even exceeds expectations, it charms generation after generation. And Didier has undeniably achieved this at Brécy. •

Practical Information

Jardins du Château de Brécy
8 Rue du Château
Hameau de Brécy
14480 Creully-sur-Seulles
Tel.: +33 (0)2 31 80 11 48
lesjardinsdebrecy@gmail.com

Opening Hours

➻ Easter (between late March and late April)–All Saints' Day (November 1):
Tuesday, Thursday, Sunday, and public holidays (and every Saturday in June): 2:30 p.m.–6:30 p.m.

➻ November 2–Easter:
Annual closure

➻ Prior appointments are required on all other days.

➻ It is recommended to send an email or telephone before visiting.

➻ **parcsetjardins.fr/jardins/84-jardins-du-chateau-de-brecy** (in French)

JARDINS du MONTPERTHUIS

✲ Chemilli,
Orne

Designed by landscape architect Philippe Dubreuil in 2010 around a fifteenth- and sixteenth-century manor house and its farm buildings, these bucolic but modern gardens feature orchards and kitchen gardens—everything required for country living.

Behind the creation of the gardens of Montperthuis lies a *jardiniste*, a rare contraction of *jardinier* (gardener) and *artiste* (artist) coined in the eighteenth century. Philippe Dubreuil has visited many gardens around the world and, more intriguingly, designed some of them. And during a prolonged stay in the Cotswolds in Britain, he fell in love with this Area of Outstanding Natural Beauty. A strong desire to put down roots and create a place of his own drew him from his native Dauphiné region into the Perche, where the landscape reminded him of the rolling hills of the Cotswolds.

The monotonous fields surrounding a dilapidated manor house and outbuildings have become an oasis of greenery.

In the heart of the bocage, the old Percheron manor house of La Pillardière, with its honey-colored stone and moss-covered roof, stood alongside a long, rectangular outhouse called a *longère*, a barn, a stable, a pigsty, a hemp oven, and a well. Bordered by a stream and a wood, the buildings had stood there peacefully since the fifteenth century and were now slowly crumbling away together in perfect harmony. The featureless fields that surrounded them would have put many people off, but not Philippe Dubreuil, who dreamed—paradoxically—of starting from a blank page while also working from historic roots.

Photographs from 2011 show a dramatic transformation. The monotonous fields surrounding a dilapidated manor house and outbuildings have become an oasis of greenery, surrounding the buildings today with a luxuriant and inventive patchwork of different rooms and garden history, bringing their beauty to life again.

Faced with the earlier "blank canvas," relieved only by a hornbeam and a hawthorn, Philippe Dubreuil first worked to create a framework, or backbone, for the five-acre (two-hectare) site, which he leveled in several places. Having planted a large avenue of elms, he designed the spaces around it. Some, such as the hellebore and magnolia garden with its two ancient statues, are half-hidden behind walls of greenery or rows of clipped box cones.

Montperthuis today possesses an English garden brimming over with peonies, viburnums, and heucheras.

In front of the house, a courtyard covering nearly an acre (4,000 square meters) was slightly raised to make a garden of clipped box squares of boxwood softened by osmanthus and muhlenbergia, and a rose garden fragrant with three hundred varieties of old rose. An octagonal fountain splashes in the center of the seventeenth-century broderie parterres, beside a medieval herb garden.

A skilled landscape designer, Philippe Dubreuil planned the perspectives and axes with meticulous care. The hedges are pierced with oeil-de-boeuf windows offering views over the bocage to the distant horizon. The gardens he has created are dotted with plant follies, fountains, and other wonderful memories of years spent traveling to gardens around the world: he wanted it all, especially the profusion of plants, flowers, foliage, and textures so admired in British gardens. Montperthuis today possesses an English garden brimming over with peonies, viburnums, and heucheras.

The central feature is the 8,500-square-foot (800-square-meter) kitchen garden, surrounded by a low wall. Between the paths lined with box hedges grow heirloom vegetables such as Jerusalem artichokes, as well as classics including tomatoes, potatoes, and lettuces, all grown without the use of pesticides. To help the harvest, he has also planted rows of perovskia, whose purple spires attract bees and insects: delighted by this bounty, they flock to pollinate and fertilize the fruit trees and vegetables.

Beside the kitchen garden is a greenhouse sheltering citrus trees, seedlings, and a cactus collection. More than five hundred trees and two thousand shrubs grace the gardens, including Japanese cherries, oaks, and limes. Following the traditional plan, the formality of the gardens around the house softens into tumbling combinations of perennials and grasses before merging into the bocage.

A conservatory orchard of cider and dessert apple trees forms an extension to a more formal orchard of cordon apple trees and espalier pear trees, which define and punctuate the space.

The gardens of Montperthuis are constantly expanding, refining their contours and evolving. Soon, Italianate terraces will appear behind the house, as this accomplished gardener and traveler continues to straddle the hemispheres and the centuries. •

Animals, awards, and a nursery

Classed as a "Jardin Remarquable" since 2021, the Montperthuis gardens have won prizes including the Bonpland Award of Excellence and the SNHF Award for the most beautiful vegetable garden in France, both in 2015, as well as the Noé Conservation award for biodiversity. Two Vietnamese pigs, a Percheron horse, and Ouessant sheep also live at Montperthuis, where they can be admired but are not for sale, unlike the many plants in the nursery. Exhibitions, themed activities, and workshops are held in the barn. Dogs are welcome in the gardens, provided they are friendly and kept on a leash.

Practical Information

Jardins du Montperthuis
Manoir de la Pillardière
61360 Chemilli
Tel.: +33 (0)6 85 30 30 81

Opening Hours
(Gardens and nursery)

→ Mid-May–late September:
Saturday and Sunday: 2 p.m.–6 p.m.

→ Late September–mid-May:
Annual closure

→ Group tours available at other times by appointment (minimum twenty people).

→ **lesjardinsdumontperthuis.com/en**

JARDIN Jungle KARLOSTACHYS

✲ Eu,
Seine-Maritime

In the town of Eu in Normandy, Charles Boulanger acclimatizes plants that he brings back from his travels, most of them collected at high altitudes. The result is an exotic and utterly improbable jungle garden, offering visitors a unique experience.

"Calvados: land of the exotic" is a notion that might bring a smile to the faces of the locals. And yet, on the Cotentin peninsula in the west and in Seine-Maritime in the east, two gardens defy the region's not-so-temperate oceanic climate and infuse an element of exoticism into its landscapes of tranquil pastures and apple orchards.

In the west, the botanical garden at Vauville (see p. 142) displays its many plant species from the southern hemisphere amid the wild moorland and rugged cliffs. In the east, not far from Dieppe and just over half a mile (just under a kilometer) from the English Channel, lies the Karlostachys jungle garden.

The unusual name derives from "Karlos," the Slavic version of Charles, and "stachys" from the bamboo genus *Phyllostachys*, from the Greek *phyllon*, meaning leaf, and *stachys* meaning spike. Karlostachys is no pretty flower garden: it's time to pull on rubber boots and explore this dense seventeen-acre (seven-hectare) jungle of giant plants.

Karlostachys is no pretty flower garden: it's time to pull on rubber boots and explore this dense jungle of giant plants.

A wood merchant by profession, Charles Boulanger worked for a time as a guide in the bamboo plantation at Anduze in the Gard region, hence his love of bamboos. Even when he was a boy, living in the heart of the Eu national forest, he would plant anything and everything that he could. As an adult, he has traveled the world and continues to do so, from Vietnam to China, and from Australia to Chile. He loves high altitudes and has brought back all kinds of hardy seeds, which have grown tall and spread throughout his jungle. His eucalyptus trees, for instance, are not just any eucalyptus, but a variety found on Mount Buffalo in Australia that can withstand temperatures as low as minus 22°F (minus 30°C)—hardy enough to shrug off Normandy winters.

Charles Boulanger is a gardener who does no gardening, or very little. He does not prune or trim, nor does he seek to tame nature. He does not plant, he sows, collects, cultivates, then watches how his imports develop, after first studying them in situ to ensure their viability.

He will not hear of using any chemicals or fertilizers, and he accepts the inevitable losses, the plants that fight aggressively and smother each other, the ivy that scrambles through the trees, and the indomitable brambles and nettles. But amid the swarms of butterflies, bees, and mosquitoes, banana palms, tree ferns, redwood trees, ginger plants, and giant cathayas with needle-like leaves all flourish.

This luxuriant, exuberant jungle has three main areas. The arboretum, shady under its dense canopy of foliage, is home to some rare trees, including the Fitzroya, or Patagonian cypress. A native of the Andes in Chile and Argentina, this majestic tree can grow to a height of 180 feet (55 meters) and can live for millennia. The oldest known member of this unique species, growing in a Chilean national park, is estimated to be 5,484 years old. In its immense shadow, the hundreds of fir trees, redwoods, and scheffleras from Southeast Asia that also thrive in this Normandy jungle seem quite domestic in scale.

Emerging from the shadows into the light, we leave the wild tangled masses of vegetation behind to enter the mists of eucalyptus and bamboo groves, stretching up to the sky. Of the three hundred and fifty varieties of bamboo, some are dwarf trees, some are climbers, and some are giants on a daunting scale, while their canes may be red, blue, or black, and round or square in section.

In among all this profusion, Charles Boulanger knows the location of every plant and will tell you their story with passion and erudition. Between five and seven thousand species grow and compete for space in his jungle, which as a parting gesture rewards the visitor with a final garden where you feel on more familiar ground, among collections of hydrangeas, orchids, and species roses.

This unorthodox gardener also loves to breed hybrid varieties and is fiercely protective of the local hazel bushes and nettles, which provide food for many butterflies. Part of an elaborate ecosystem, like the frogs that leap out of the pond to gobble up slugs, the jungle garden is at once exotic and indigenous, carefully tended despite its apparent wildness.

As landscape designer Pascal Cribier says, "Charles Boulanger is an innovator because he's not making an ornamental garden, but a living laboratory, using species of which he has a perfect knowledge." •

Guided tours

♥ *At Karlostachys, all tours are guided by Charles Boulanger himself. Visitors have two options: a two-hour group tour, usually on Saturday afternoons, from mid-March to the end of October, or a private tour for one to five people. Both must be reserved in advance (by SMS).*

Practical Information

Jardin Jungle Karlostachys
Route de Beaumont (between the Ferme de Beaumont and the Briga archeological site)
76260 Eu
Tel.: +33 (0)6 23 75 19 73
charles.boulanger@yahoo.fr

Opening Hours

(Guided group tours only)

➸ Mid-March–late October:
Daily from 2:30 p.m. (reservation recommended but not mandatory)
See website for exact tour times and for tours in English.

➸ Late October–mid-March:
Annual closure

➸ In the event of strong winds, tours may be cancelled.

➸ No direct vehicle access and site inaccessible to wheelchair users and families with strollers.

➸ Walking boots and waterproof clothing recommended.

➸ **jardinjungle.com**

BOIS des MOUTIERS

✵ Varengeville-sur-Mer,
Seine-Maritime

One of the finest examples in France of the Arts and Crafts movement, the Bois des Moutiers is the fruit of a unique collaboration between world renowned architect Edwin Lutyens and celebrated landscape designer Gertrude Jekyll. It has recently undergone a complete renovation program aiming to respect the spirit of the original.

The village of Varengeville-sur-Mer, perched on the chalk cliffs of the Alabaster Coast, facing the shores of England over the waters of the English Channel, has attracted artists for centuries. In the nineteenth century, it welcomed influential figures from the Arts and Crafts movement, whose origins lay in the rejection of the Industrial Revolution that had transformed Victorian Britain.

In 1884, Monet made seven paintings of Varengeville's beautiful church of Saint Valéry. This ancient building has stained-glass windows by the artist Raoul Ubac, as well as one by Georges Braque, who lived in the village for four months each year and is buried in the church graveyard. His words are inscribed on the wall above his gravestone looking out to sea: "I am far more interested in being in unison with nature than in copying it." Other creative figures drawn here include the painter Joan Miró, who began his *Constellations* series here, and the writer Louis Aragon. But before these artists, the remarkable light, sea air, white cliffs, and gentle landscape had seduced the art-loving banker Guillaume Mallet and his wife Adélaïde Grunelius, who decided to buy an estate here at the turn of the nineteenth century.

Four generations of the Mallet family succeeded one another at the Bois des Moutiers, sharing a love of the place and an admiration for the work of their forebears. Eventually, however, the responsibilities and complications involved in maintaining the immense estate persuaded them to part with it. Acquired in 2020 by Jérôme and Sophie Seydoux, the gardens at the Bois des Moutiers have been renovated throughout by landscape architect Madison Cox, respecting their original vocation and appearance, their harmony and simplicity of form, as well as the symbiotic relationship between the house and nature, and between the occupants and the surrounding countryside.

The estate consists of a stone and brick house with steep, tiled roofs and tall windows, surrounded by formal gardens and a beautiful English-style landscape garden behind the house, designed and planted by Guillaume Mallet, in the hanging valley leading down to the sea. By 1898, Guillaume Mallet had given up his career as a cavalry officer to devote himself wholeheartedly, along with Adélaïde, to the creation of the house and gardens, and the couple was driven by aesthetic, scientific, and spiritual ambitions inspired by their theosophical beliefs.

The architectural elements follow theosophical principles, and consequently a walk through the grounds is rich in references and symbols. The golden section is used throughout to establish a symbiotic relationship between the house, garden, and park, and to create pure harmony and simplicity. Committed to this ambitious and pioneering project that was both aesthetic and spiritual, the Mallets turned to a young and brilliant English architect, Edwin Lutyens, and the renowned landscape designer Gertrude Jekyll. Their collaboration would leave a lasting mark on the history of garden design.

Conceived as a journey of introduction, inspired by the writings of the English gardener and writer William Robinson, the gardens were laid out as green rooms that communicated with each other, echoing the rooms of the house and acting as an extension of it. Covering five and twenty acres (two and eight hectares) respectively, the gardens and parkland follow the classic principle of a gradual transition from a highly structured landscape to one that is almost completely natural.

Laid out in terraces and enclosed by walls, the green rooms feature formal French broderie parterres in clipped box, a white garden, rose beds, topiary, and the famous mixed borders—the first to be planted in France. The signature style of Gertrude Jekyll, who was a trained painter and an expert in color, can be seen in the combinations of hues and textures inspired by a medieval palette, and in the graduated composition of the flower beds. All the green rooms are connected by flights of steps or long pergolas clothed in wisteria and climbing roses. The former kitchen garden has been transformed into a rose garden, while a superb grassy path is lined by huge bell-shaped topiary.

As the land slopes downwards, so more exotic species appear, thriving in the acidic soil here—a rarity in the Pays de Caux. Planted by Guillaume Mallet and inspired not only by Gertrude Jekyll and William Robinson but also by Pre-Raphaelite paintings, as well as Claude Lorrain and Nicolas Poussin, the park, too, is a work of art. Mallet also observed the Arts and Crafts principle of acclimatizing large numbers of exotic species and mixing them in with native varieties. Chinese azaleas, Chilean eucryphias, tree ferns, and giant rhododendrons standing thirty feet (ten meters) tall lead to the magnolia garden. Further on, through a succession of clearings, the landscape park merges into nature and views of the sea.

At the Bois des Moutiers, visitors wander through woodland glades of venerable oaks, black pines, and hornbeams, with, above them, the spreading branches of a cedar of Lebanon or the scarlet fall foliage of a rare Japanese maple. The last meadow sloping gently down to the sea is filled with perennials, with a view back up the sweeping grassy slopes fringed by stately hydrangeas in a palette that changes with the seasons. Further up and slightly to the right, the tall white cliffs and the belfry of the church of Saint-Valéry rise into the clear sky, a stained-glass window by Braque glimmers in the light, and a painting by Monet seems to take shape before our eyes. •

Practical Information

Bois des Moutiers
46 Route de l'Église
76119 Varengeville-sur-Mer

Opening Hours

(Guided group tours only)

- May, June, and August:
Tuesday–Saturday: 10 a.m.–11:45 a.m.
- September–November:
Friday and Saturday: 10 a.m.–11:45 a.m.
- July, and November–April:
Annual closures

- Timed tickets must be purchased on the garden's official website
- **boisdesmoutiers.com/en**

Nouvelle-Aquitaine

Jardins du Manoir d'Eyrignac, Salignac-Eyvigues • Dordogne
Parc de Majolan, Blanquefort • Gironde

JARDINS du Manoir d'EYRIGNAC

✲ Salignac-Eyvigues, Dordogne

The gardens surrounding the manor house of Eyrignac, set in the beautiful landscape of the Périgord Noir, unfold over twenty-five acres (ten hectares). Showcasing the art of topiary in breathtaking variety, they include green sculptures, green rooms, and broderie parterres, and the perfectly and meticulously formed shapes create a magical universe.

So dense and dark are the ancient evergreen holm oak forests that cast an atmospheric misty hue over the region's rolling hills and valleys that they have endowed the Périgord Noir region—home also to black truffles—with its name. Amid this wild beauty, just a few miles from Sarlat, stands a beacon of sunlit parterres and honey-colored stone: the Manoir d'Eyrignac and its gardens. A historical and botanical jewel of the department, it has been listed as a historic monument since 1986.

The original small castle on this site, dating from the early medieval period, was destroyed by the troops of Louis II de Bourbon, known as Le Grand Condé. The Manoir d'Artaban was built on its ruins in the seventeenth and eighteenth centuries; it was a more comfortable, bourgeois residence featuring large mullioned windows and a square *pigeonnier* (dovecote), with the golden limestone walls and stone-tiled roofs so characteristic of Périgord architecture. Over the last five hundred years, no fewer than twenty-two generations of the same family have lived in this gracious manor house, with its monumental stone fireplaces, terra-cotta tiles, exposed beams, antique furniture, and numerous family portraits.

The first gardens were laid out in the eighteenth century, in the formal geometric manner that became known as the French style, and that was inspired by the contemporary vogue for the formality of Italian Renaissance gardens. In the nineteenth century, following the changing whims of fashion, the geometric gardens were replaced with a landscape garden in the English style, thus completely losing their formal identity.

In 1965, Gilles Sermadiras, the father of the present owner, decided that he wanted to recreate the gardens in the spirit of the eighteenth century. Inspired by this vision, he embarked on meticulous detective work throughout the grounds, unearthing traces of the eighteenth-century, from steps to low walls as well as the sites of former ponds. Then he personally redesigned the garden that he had long dreamed of. Today, his son, Patrick Sermadiras, is keen to preserve and pay homage to his father's legacy, and maintains the unmistakably French charm of the gardens with rigor and passion.

In 2005, the gardens were awarded the "Jardin Remarquable" label from the French Ministry of Culture, and its seven green rooms, renowned for their intricate topiary sculptures and parterres, now occupy twenty-five acres (ten hectares) of the huge five-hundred-acre (two-hundred-hectare) estate.

Here, the art of topiary has no limits in its forms of expression. Yew, box, cypress, elm, hornbeam, and ivy are clipped and coaxed into geometric forms—balls, cubes, cones, pyramids, spirals, straight hedges, and broderie parterres—as well as figures, including a charming gathering of farmyard animals. Each shape or sculpture—and there are some three hundred of them altogether—is trimmed day after day using shears, with a precision at which visitors can only marvel.

The seven gardens all showcase their unique features in a subtle palette of gradations of green, punctuated with roses, herbaceous perennials, rare vegetables, and spring bulbs. Lying at the heart of the estate is the Jardin Français (French Garden), a formal parterre *à la française*, with topiary and clipped hedges, creating depth and perspectives in shades of green against a sweep of green lawn and straight paths in the manner of André Le Nôtre.

The Jardin Blanc (White Garden), created in 2000, adds a note of airy lightness to the gardens, while also complementing the French Garden with its perspectives and clipped greenery. The purity and elegance traditionally associated with white gardens is created by five hundred fragrant white roses, including repeat-flowering "Opalia" and "Madame Alfred Carrière," together with narcissi, tulips, hyacinths, gauras, hydrangeas, salvias, and dahlias, according to the season. From here you can stroll along the one-hundred-and-ten-yard (one-hundred-meter) long Allée des Charmes (Hornbeam Alley), lined with hornbeams clipped into curtains of greenery, and the Allée des Vases (Vase Alley), punctuated with yew balls in carved stone urns.

Here, the art of topiary has no limits in its forms of expression.

From springtime on, the cutting garden is filled with color, as tulips, alliums, lilies, lupins, alstroemerias, and dahlias succeed each other. Reached through an avenue of weeping cedars, the kitchen garden is laid out in geometric squares hedged with box and features heritage varieties of parsnips and artichokes mingling with carrots, sage, thyme, and rosemary. Companion plantings of colorful marigolds, carnations, and nasturtiums keep pests at bay and attract pollinating insects.

Finally, in the lush Jardin des Sources (Spring-Fed Garden), laid out by Patrick Sermadiras in 2013 to celebrate the natural springs that are such an important feature of the estate, ponds are filled with water lilies and surrounded by royal ferns and yellow flag irises. Newly created square gardens focus on pollinating plants and grasses, with insect hotels to support biodiversity within the gardens. The central path, lined with fruit trees, leads naturally to the Verger de la Rotonde (Rotunda Orchard), an orchard of over fifty varieties of apples, pears, damsons, and cherries. •

Picnics and shop

♥ *Every Monday evening in July and August, the gardens welcome young and old alike for its "white picnics," with dancing to tunes courtesy of a DJ, singing, cocktails, and ice cream. Luminous ambiences and a firework display dazzle the gardens and guests. The only condition to participate in the festivities is that everyone must wear white. And to take home a memento of this memorable visit, the park's shop offers an array of scented candles, chairs, gardening tools, teacups, fridge magnets, fans, and card games.*

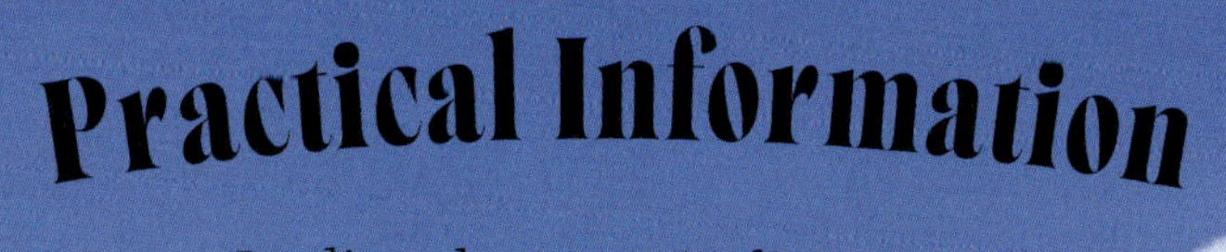

Practical Information

Jardins du Manoir d'Eyrignac
24590 Salignac-Eyvigues
Tel.: +33 (0)5 53 28 99 71
contact@eyrignac.com

Opening Hours

Open daily throughout the year (including public holidays):

➛ April–September:
9:30 a.m.–7 p.m. (10 a.m. in April)

➛ October:
10 a.m.– 6 p.m.

➛ November–March:
10:30 a.m.–12:30 p.m., 2:30 p.m.–nightfall

➛ **eyrignac.com/en**

PARC de MAJOLAN

✲ Blanquefort, Gironde

This beautifully restored park was designed as a nineteenth-century folly, laid out on former marshland. A large lake is the central feature, with walking routes through woods, over mysterious bridges, and past dramatic caves and grottoes, offering visitors a journey of discovery.

It all began when Joseph Prom, a wealthy colonial merchant of questionable character, acquired the Dulamon estate in the Gironde and, in 1865, built a château on the ruins of a medieval fortress. He wanted it to look like the palace of Fontainebleau, and the result was undeniably impressive. Designed by the Bordeaux architect Jules Laffargue, the principal façade, in honey-colored stone, measured two hundred feet (sixty-three meters) in length and was flanked by a pair of pavilions, and the ensemble boasted seven roofs topped by a dome. The estate, including vineyards and a "wonderfully laid out park," covered one hundred and forty acres (fifty-six hectares).

When Prom and his wife died at the turn of the twentieth century, their heiress married Jean Gustave Piganeau, a banker with big ambitions and an even bigger fortune, rather like a nineteenth-century banker in a novel by Balzac or Zola. Bordering the estate was some stagnant marshland, which he lost no time in buying up. He wanted a garden—one that would be romantic, baroque, dazzling, picturesque; a modern creation that would impress his peers and might even be talked about in Paris, the eternal bugbear of the provinces. What else was a fortune for, after all?

According to the eighteenth-century landscape architect Gabriel Thouin, romantic gardens inspired by English landscapes should feature "very varied ground, elevations, and, in their contours, lawns, carpets of flowers, masses of shrubs, woods, tall trees, and water in the various states in which it is found in nature." Not to mention columns, grottoes, statues, and ruins, or any number of "decorative follies." There was a lot of work to do, and there was also—as underpins any *folie de grandeur*—a genuine desire for beauty. And so it transpired that the pretty commune of Blanquefort, on the outskirts of Bordeaux, had to endure major works for the following ten years.

The Jalle river was diverted to create a lake covering ten acres (four hectares), surrounded by a promenade. Inventive craftsmen and specialists in making rockeries built artificial caves from lime, canyons, rock bridges, fountains, faux ruins, and meandering paths planted with rare and exotic species. And so Piganeau had his romantic park at Majolan.

Unfortunately, Piganeau went on to lose his fortune, and the château and estate were sold and then more or less abandoned. In the 1950s, a *guinguette* or open-air café sprang up briefly in the gardens, and much later the château would become home to Les Apprentis d'Auteuil, an organization working with disadvantaged young people.

In 1975, the park was bought by the municipality. In 1984, it was opened to the public, and in 2007, its initial restoration was complete. Now a hugely popular spot for people in the Bordeaux area, it offers fifty acres (twenty hectares) of long walks scented by native and exotic species, with the magnificent lake as its centerpiece, reflecting the surrounding foliage and grottoes. The caves carved and excavated into its banks share the space with expansive lawns for picnics and relaxation. Rocky promontories offer views of swans, mallards, and moorhens gliding among the water lilies, lotuses, and flag irises. Herons and kingfishers can also be spotted, watched closely by the bats that shelter in cavities in the rocks.

The maze of caves, galleries, and tunnels are currently undergoing renovation work, but visitors can still admire their outlines and baroque architecture as they cross the rock bridge—an artful stone and concrete construction that mimics a natural rock arch.

After this, winding paths lead off in different directions, for visitors to explore as they wish. Some lead into the woods, under the shade of venerable oaks, planes, cedars, sequoias, and hornbeams. Bamboo groves make a striking sight on the fringes of the woods. The paths twist and turn, and just as you begin to feel slightly and delightfully lost, a sunny wildflower meadow suddenly opens up before you, bordered by elegant parterres. In this theatrical succession of scenery and greenery, of nature reinvented and nature artificially created, the enterprising Piganeau would surely find all the romanticism he so craved.

The paths twist and turn, and just as you begin to feel slightly and delightfully lost, a sunny wildflower meadow suddenly opens up before you, bordered by elegant parterres.

In spring, the lawns are fringed by beds of tulips and daffodils, while the broader paths are scattered with the pink and white petals of magnolias and Japanese cherries. The air is perfumed with the intoxicating fragrance of wisterias and lilacs.

In summer, old roses, lavender, and blue and mauve hydrangeas add color, and visitors can find relief from the summer sun in the shady woodland gardens planted with ferns, hostas, and Japanese anemones.

Awarded the "Jardin Remarquable" label by the French Ministry of Culture and listed as a historic monument since 2007, Parc de Majolan takes visitors on a journey through clearings and meadows, woodland and rocky belvederes, sunlight and shadow. And there is also plenty for children to enjoy. In the heart of the park is a playground with a double zip line, and, further on, wooden structures decorated with totems and carved animals invite children of all ages to play at being in the wild west. Meanwhile, beneath the cherry trees and Japanese maples, beside the lake or near a fountain, among the azaleas and camellias, numerous benches have been thoughtfully placed to welcome weary walkers. •

Practical Information

Parc de Majolan
Avenue du Général-de-Gaulle
33290 Blanquefort
Tel.: +33 (0)5 56 95 50 95

Opening Hours

➻ April–September:
Open daily: 8 a.m.–8:30 p.m.

➻ October–March:
Open daily, except Tuesday: 8:30 a.m.–6 p.m.

➻ Self-guided tours and free access.

➻ **ville-blanquefort.fr/activites-et-sorties/prendre-l-air/parc-de-majolan** (in French)

Occitanie

Jardins des Martels, Giroussens • Tarn

JARDINS des MARTELS

✲ Giroussens, Tarn

These unique Asian-inspired English landscape gardens are famed for their remarkable collection of lotuses and other aquatic plants. A dreamy and thought-provoking park to discover at one's leisure.

Marie-Thérèse and André Reynier have always loved flowers—a passion they nevertheless pushed to the back of their minds for a time. In 1969, they decided to go into farming, so they left their native Aveyron and bought land some twenty miles (thirty kilometers) north of Toulouse, in the little village of Giroussens, renowned for its pottery and ceramics.

There, they planted corn and raised ducks. For their waterfowl they made a pond, on which a few water lilies quietly appeared. Reminded of their love for flowers, they then lost no time in landscaping the area around the farmhouse, making broad grassy paths and adding color with beautiful flower beds.

By 1975, their green spaces had flourished so much that the farm had metamorphosed into a veritable park. The couple entered the local Fermes Fleuries du Tarn competition, which aimed to find the prettiest flower gardens attached to a farm. And they won—not just once, but several times.

Their son Frédéric, who was born into this haven of color and greenery, chose to study horticulture. After graduation he wanted to open a plant nursery, and he knew that the gardens would make an ideal showcase for his plants. Friends, neighbors, and other visitors could not conceal their admiration for the flower beds and water gardens, especially after an article appeared in the local press. And gradually the idea took hold: what if they opened the gardens to the public? In 1994, the Jardins des Martels were born. They were an immediate success, with visitor numbers growing exponentially year on year.

The Reyniers were encouraged by this success. Always seeking to expand and improve the gardens—which today extend over eight and a half acres (three and a half hectares)—they have never been short of ideas or ambition. They created a greenhouse for exotic plants; a mini-farm with donkeys, chickens, goats, and other animals; more ponds for waterlilies and lotuses, turtles and fish; and even more flower beds, adding color and interest, and prolonging the exceptionally long flowering season.

In 2005, Frédéric met Lionel Dominique, whose communication skills have helped to shape the gardens' remarkable success. Frédéric and Lionel started to travel the world together, and Bali in particular became a place of special inspiration for them. In 2009, they installed a lotus temple, which is reached by Japanese stepping stones, adding a Balinese Joglo, or gazebo, and a staircase waterfall a few years later. A Mediterranean garden was then created, using dry-stone construction and featuring yuccas, agapanthus, and trachelospermum (star jasmine), followed more recently by a little Chinese temple in the Indonesian garden. Meanwhile statues of the Buddha, plump and contented, smile serenely in the shady groves, and a venerable 270-year-old olive tree presides sagely over the expanding gardens and plant nursery, where visitors can buy plants cultivated from those that flourish in the gardens and browse a unique selection of perennials, grasses and shrubs, climbers, roses, and especially hydrangeas and aquatic plants.

For Frédéric Reynier, this multifaceted garden forms a single entity with gradually changing atmospheres, which visitors can experience on a walk that flows like the water that underpins it. The 140-yard (130-meter) long canal that winds its way between magnolias, wisterias, and viburnums makes a delightful prelude to the many ponds filled with spectacular displays of giant water lilies and delicate lotus flowers. An aquatic greenhouse shelters water lilies in every shade, as

well as bignonias, jasmines, passion flowers, daturas, and banana palms.

Every season at the Jardins des Martels offers its own delights for visitors to enjoy. In spring, the landscaping of the paths and ponds, woodland, and flower beds and the architecture of the garden buildings can be fully appreciated as the gardens stir into life. Daffodils and tulips add spots of brilliant color beneath the clear blues of ceanothus and the whites and pinks of flowering cherries and viburnums. The lacy foliage of Japanese maples, in every shade from freshest green to deepest purple, flutters in the lightest breeze, and in May the wisterias and old-fashioned roses begin to scent the air. While irises and peonies bloom for their brief but sumptuous flowering seasons, the ponds are studded with waterlilies and fringed with drifts of yellow flags.

Summer brings an explosion of color and plant life, notably with the gardens' magnificent hydrangeas in many different varieties, agapanthus in brilliant shades of blue, climbing and rambling roses, and arching pink and white gauras. But the star turn is undoubtedly the lotus flowers—a sight to behold as their fragrant pink and white blooms unfold above carpets of waterlily-like leaves. The hydrangeas bloom on into late summer, to be joined by late-flowering ceanothus, the crumpled, silky petals of hibiscus, and dainty fuchsias.

In fall, the low rays of the sun outline the sculptural forms of the lotus seed heads, and the golden light gilds the glowing foliage colors that become ever more intense as the temperature drops. Mists cling to the ponds and streams, and lend a dreamy aura to the silhouettes of trees and shrubs.

In fall, the low rays of the sun outline the sculptural forms of the lotus seed heads, and the golden light gilds the glowing foliage colors that become ever more intense.

From the romanticism of English rose gardens and peonies to the warmth of the Mediterranean garden and the exoticism of Bali, the Jardins des Martels are a feast for the senses and an invitation to explore a constantly evolving succession of compositions and perspectives. Classified as a "Jardin Remarquable" by the French Ministry of Culture, the gardens are now one of the most visited spots in the Tarn region, and are frequently cited as one of France's most beautiful gardens. •

Art, literature, and music among the plants

♥ *As innovative as it is aesthetic in its approach, the park features flower beds dotted with unobtrusive barcodes containing horticultural information, while a smartphone app invites visitors to luxuriate in readings of texts by great writers on gardens and plants while relaxing on the lawns. The gardens also host regular art exhibitions by painters, sculptors, and ceramists, as well as jazz evenings, yoga sessions, and tours of the impressive nursery greenhouses.*

Practical Information

Jardins des Martels
391 Route des Martels
81500 Giroussens
Tel.: +33 (0)5 63 41 61 42
contact@jardinsdesmartels.com

Opening Hours

➳ April and September:
Open daily (including public holidays):
1:30 p.m.–6 p.m.

➳ May–August:
Open daily (including public holidays):
10 a.m.–6 p.m.

➳ October:
Wednesday, Saturday, and Sunday:
1:30 p.m.–6 p.m. (open daily in second half of October, weather permitting)

➳ November–March:
Annual closure

➳ Final admissions one hour before closing.

➳ **jardinsdesmartels.com/en**

Pays de la Loire

Parc Oriental de Maulévrier, Maulévrier • Maine-et-Loire
Prieuré de Vauboin, Beaumont-sur-Dême • Sarthe
Jardins de William Christie, Thiré • Vendée

PARC Oriental de MAULÉVRIER

Maulévrier, Maine-et-Loire

Created as a curiosity following the 1900 World's Fair, the garden at Maulévrier was later recognized by Japanese academics as an authentic recreation of an eighteenth-century Edo period stroll garden. Here, nature symbolizes the passage of time and the seasons represent the cycle of life.

The 1900 World's Fair in Paris—the most ambitious ever held—was a proud, inventive, and lavish celebration of "the achievements of the century" and the astonishing progress they had yielded. It also set out to promote the brotherhood of nations. More than forty countries participated, vowing loyalty to one another amid the splendor of their national pavilions—though none of the emperors and presidents, many of them cousins, could have predicted the catastrophic collapse of that brotherhood a mere fourteen years later.

When it closed after 212 days, this great celebration nonetheless left behind memories of wildly modern extravaganzas, such as the "moving sidewalk," an ancestor of the escalator, which ran along the Seine for nearly two miles (three kilometers). It also coincided with the opening of the first Métro line, from Porte Maillot to Porte de Vincennes, and would give Parisians the enduring legacy of the Petit Palais; the Grand Palais; the Pont Alexandre III bridge, symbol of cordial Franco-Russian relations; and, among many other wonders, a garden in the oriental style in the Anjou region.

Alexandre Marcel, the celebrated architect who created the garden, was a passionate Orientalist. Like so many of his fellow architects during the Belle Époque, he was irresistibly drawn to the so-called "exotic," and in particular to Japonism. Without ever setting foot on the Asian continent, he gained a reputation as an expert on those distant lands, and was commissioned to design structures for the World's Fair, including the Cambodian Pavilion and a Japanese Tower.

It was against this background of imperialistic zeal that Marcel married the daughter of a wealthy industrialist, Eugène Bergère, owner of the Château de Maulévrier. Built on the site of a fortified castle in the nineteenth century, the château was set in more than seventy acres (twenty-nine hectares) of grounds. Alexandre Marcel became the estate architect and, with the help of the head gardener, Alphonse Duveau, he set about transforming the gardens into a "Japanese landscape." They excavated a lake, widened the Moine river, laid out a riverside walk, planted large numbers of trees, pruned them in traditional fashion into cloud shapes, and scattered among them elements that had featured in the World's Fair, including temples, Khmer statues, and lanterns. In spring, the cherry trees came into blossom, and visitors admired the graceful—and at that time completely unfamiliar—aesthetics of the gardens.

In 1928, Marcel died, and the gardens fell into a period of neglect. Following the sale of the estate in 1945, it was abandoned and forgotten for nearly forty years. Then, in 1980, the local government bought it, and Jean-Louis Belouard, the local mayor, had it listed as a natural site of national importance, while local residents formed teams of volunteers to embark on the huge task of clearing the vegetation. In 1982, an association was set up, volunteers and professionals joined forces, and work on the garden rapidly gained momentum. Three years later, the garden opened to the public. Before long, it was recognized by three professors from Japanese horticultural colleges in Tokyo and Niigata as a classic Edo period (seventeenth–nineteenth centuries) stroll garden. It is now the largest Japanese garden in Europe. Awarded the label of "Jardin Remarquable" by the French Ministry of Culture in 2004, Maulévrier celebrated its fortieth anniversary as a public garden in 2025.

In this landscape, meticulously composed according to traditional Japanese aesthetic principles, strolling and contemplation signify a journey through the ages of life, symbolized by the changing seasons: spring is youth, summer adulthood, fall old age, with the wisdom that accompanies it, and winter rest before new growth. The flow of the river from east to west, meanwhile, symbolizes the passage of the sun through the sky from sunrise to sunset. More than four hundred species of plants mark the unfolding of the seasons with a changing palette: the pink and white of cherry blossom and azaleas in spring give way in summer to a tapestry of greens punctuated by the blues and mauves of hydrangeas, and finally, in fall, the flaming scarlet and bronze of maples and the brilliant gold of ginkgos.

Five essential components make up the garden: water, stone, plants, structures, and circulation. Among its structures, sculptures, and plants are traditional features of Japanese gardens, including the *torii* (tall open gates marking the transition from the worldly to the sacred); semicircular bridges, also sacred in character; and *ishidôro* (Japanese lanterns), all unique and symbolizing knowledge and the human presence. There are also sculpted turtles and cranes representing the complementary energies of sea and sky, yin and yang; cloud-pruned trees; and *shimenawa*—ropes that signify the presence of *kami* (Japanese spirits).

Throughout the garden, windows in the greenery and cloud-pruned trees are positioned to offer views that gradually reveal the scenery, with symbolic depictions of the rocky coasts, mountains, islands, and waterfalls of Japanese landscapes, both real and mythical. •

Nocturnal walks and monthly festivities

♥ *Following the Japanese custom, the garden proposes nocturnal walks by lantern light, accompanied by readings of haiku and Japanese traditional tales, providing an opportunity to discover the subtle and mysterious beauty of the garden in a different light. Maulévrier also has a pretty tearoom with a shady terrace bordered by a pond filled with koi carp, a shop specializing in Asian and Japanese products, and a specialist plant nursery and bonsai collection. There are festivities held every month in the garden, the most famous being* Hanami *in March, when the cherry trees are in blossom, and* Bonsai Shō *in June, dedicated to bonsai enthusiasts and offering displays, workshops, demonstrations, and lectures.*

Practical Information

Parc Oriental de Maulévrier
Place de la Mairie
49360 Maulévrier
Tel.: +33 (0)2 41 55 50 14

Opening Hours

➳ Mid-March–mid-November:
Open daily (including public holidays): opening hours vary, so check website before your visit or ring ahead.

➳ Mid-November–mid-March:
Annual closure

➳ Final admissions one hour before closing.

➳ Self-guided tours, and guided tours available at no extra cost every Sunday and on public holidays at 2:30 p.m. (provided no other events are taking place that day).

➳ **parc-oriental.com/en**

PRIEURÉ de VAUBOIN

✲ Beaumont-sur-Dême, Sarthe

This jewel of a garden featuring clipped box labyrinths covered in white narcissi and showered with cherry blossoms surrounds a small seventeenth-century priory. On the steep slope behind, a wildly imaginative forest of wild box has been clipped over the last thirty years into a myriad of unique shapes.

For feudal lords in medieval times, the *hortus conclusus*, or enclosed garden, laid out at the foot of fortified towers and crenellated walls, served a practical purpose, offering exercise and delights for all the senses in a dangerous and troubled world.

First mentioned in the *Song of Songs*, the *hortus conclusus* is the earliest ancestor of Western gardens. A recurring motif in European religious art, it was linked symbolically with the Virgin Mary by many early mystics, and in the cloisters of monasteries it became emblematic of a "perfect life in God." Combining the idea of paradise with an enduring nostalgia for the Garden of Eden, this ideal world was shielded from the evils and temptations of the outside world by hedges, walls, or fences.

Thierry Juge wanted green and only green—the color of the heart chakra—with touches of white for purity.

In 1991, Thierry Juge, a successful executive based in Paris, was seeking to "withdraw from the world," when he found his future nirvana in the rolling countryside midway between Tours and Le Mans. Located—to its new owner's great delight—in the middle of nowhere, the seventeenth-century priory is

small and spare, the epitome of simplicity with its unadorned gray stone walls and steep slate roof.

In keeping with monastic tradition, the first garden—his *hortus conclusus*—is divided into four parts: a vegetable garden and orchard on one side, and on the other a labyrinth, the spiritual heart of the garden symbolizing the path of life, and a cloister, represented here by a single box tree behind the priory. But first he built the most essential element: a wall to enclose the garden, using stacked chestnut logs topped with vine clippings and interspersed with scented roses. Within the walls, a quince tree, a walnut tree, and an ash tree flourish, and two gunneras shade a clear stream with their giant rhubarb-like leaves.

Everything here is about geometry and perfect alignment.

Everything here is about geometry and perfect alignment: the squares are bisected by diagonals of topiary pyramids and the graphic lines of cinder paths; formal parterres and the clipped box of the labyrinth evoke the classic formality of a French garden; an orchard of cherry trees is punctuated with large box balls set on the diagonal. Only a scattering of white narcissi, forget-me-nots, and clematis add spots of light and color to this green canvas. Thierry Juge wanted green and only green—the color of the heart chakra—with touches of white for purity.

This austere paradise was completed in 1996. Then, ten years later, Thierry Juge acquired the steep slope rising behind the priory and set about clearing the tangle of woodland that clothed it, only to discover a thicket of hundreds of wild box trees, reaching heights of several feet.

Thierry has loved box ever since he was a boy. For him it is an extraordinary evergreen plant, easy to prune into an infinite variety of shapes, and a symbol of eternity. After discovering this enchanted forest, he spent four long years observing it, imagining a shape for each box tree. When he finally started pruning, the results were astonishing. This upper garden, as baroque as the lower one is austere, endows the whole ensemble with a unique and idiosyncratic charm.

The box trees were initially cut back completely, then pruned constantly with Japanese shears, to reveal their inner selves in all shapes and sizes. Some even resemble figures with distinct personalities to whom Thierry has given names. He has whitewashed some of the trunks to accentuate their angles, while on others he has clipped the new growth right back to encourage the foliage to clothe them entirely. Drawing inspiration from his travels, as well as from photographers whose work he admires and, above all, from artists such as Miró and Giacometti, he is guided by nature and his intuition, and spends his days sculpting plants according to his imagination.

Awarded the label of "Jardin Remarquable" by the French Ministry of Culture in 2014, the garden won the Prix de l'Art du Jardin in 2020—much to the surprise of Thierry Juge, who declares that he never expected the garden to attract any visitors, let alone to win any prizes. •

By appointment only

♥ *The idiosyncratic nature of the garden is reflected in its equally original visiting arrangements. Visits are by appointment only and must be made by telephone in advance. There is a modest entrance fee, but you can also visit for free in exchange for an hour of weeding.*

Practical Information

Prieuré de Vauboin
72340 Beaumont-sur-Dême
Tel.: +33 (0)2 43 79 04 23
contact@leprieuredevauboin.fr

Opening Hours

- Early April–early October:
Tours available by appointment only.

- Mid-October–end March:
Annual closure

- **leprieuredevauboin.fr** (in French)

JARDINS de William CHRISTIE

✵ Thiré, Vendée

It was in 1985 that the internationally renowned conductor and harpsichordist William Christie fell in love with this abandoned estate. Starting from scratch, he has since created a series of spaces inspired by the art of formal French gardening in its eighteenth-century heyday, combining baroque fantasy with rigorous classicism. This "musical garden" is now also a performance space.

William Christie is famed for playing and conducting the neglected musical masterpieces of the seventeenth and eighteenth centuries on period instruments. He has won many accolades for reviving the compositions and reputations of composers including Marc-Antoine Charpentier, Jean-Philippe Rameau, and Jean-Baptiste Lully, and for bringing their music to a wider audience.

His other passion is perhaps less well known. The son of an American musician and architect, he developed an early love of nature and learned the basics of gardening from his parents and grandparents. After studying art history at Harvard and music at Yale, he left the United States to move to the UK and France—a country that his parents held dear.

In 1985, he set off in his red Volkswagen Beetle to give a couple of performances in the Vendée region, which proved a great success. On the way back, the sight of a large and abandoned farmhouse on the outskirts of the village of Thiré brought him to a halt. He gazed at the neglected fields that lay all around it. For a long time he had been wanting to create a garden, and more particularly a space in which could express his passion for classicism, symmetry, and topiary. Most of all, he wanted to start it from scratch. Forty years later, William Christie's exquisite gardens, combining English, Italian, and French influences, bear witness to both his imagination and his erudition.

Having visited and studied many gardens around the world, William Christie has amassed a wealth of knowledge to inspire the garden of his dreams, a "musical garden." It is, in his own words, "an artist's garden. Whimsical, full of poetic license. . . . When I think of this garden, I think of the music I love."

Also known as the Jardins du Bâtiment, Christie's garden has been awarded the "Jardin Remarquable" label by the French Ministry of Culture. Eclectic, imaginative, and filled with personal touches, it is nonetheless imbued throughout with the spirit of classicism and the baroque. Covering thirty acres (twelve hectares), it consists largely of trees, shrubs, lawns, and topiary, with spring bulbs and flowering plants in pots. For the most part unchanged in appearance in summer and winter alike, it bears out Edith Wharton's description of the gardens of the great Italian villas: "The Italian garden does not exist for its flowers; its flowers exist for it; they are a late and infrequent adjunct to its beauties."

Christie started with the Cour d'Honneur (Main Courtyard), which at first—with its clipped box broderie parterres featuring musical clefs, and its hedges of limes and hornbeams—evokes the French formal tradition in garden design. On closer inspection, however, it reveals more eclectic influences in its Dutch box pyramids and its yew buttresses, climbing roses on the walls, and rustic chestnut pergola with chinoiserie motifs, all of which, as William Christie has observed, take inspiration from the twentieth-century Arts and Crafts aesthetic.

The reflecting pool beckons us into a Versailles-inspired reverie. Lines of lofty plane trees above a hornbeam hedge are reflected in the mirror-like waters of this long pool, leading the eye to a rocaille tableau set against a clipped hornbeam colonnade at the far end. One of the gardens' most iconic features, the pool captures the essence of the magnificent water features that are so emblematic of French seventeenth-century garden design. In summer, it shimmers with the lights of the Dans les Jardins de William Christie festival, when it becomes the magical setting for floating performances of music and dance, echoing the most glittering celebrations of the Grand Siècle.

The cloister pays homage to an essential feature in the iconography of European enclosed gardens, while also including personal touches. A "Madame Alfred Carrière" climbing rose perfumes the air in this sheltered spot. The terrace and parterre take advantage of the gentle slope down to the river to create a spectacular

view over the gardens, while evergreen columns of star jasmine (*Trachelospermum jasminoides*) scent the air in summer. In the Pinède (Pine Grove), umbrella pines shade a lawn scattered with antique stelae, creating an atmosphere redolent of Italian gardens and a classical Arcadia, while in spring the grass under the tall cypresses is carpeted with white tulips and narcissi.

The yew theater is a fantastical creation, "a horticultural caprice," in Christie's words, designed to "depart from the more sober and formal parts of the ensemble adjacent to it." A flamboyant extravaganza of arabesques in yew, box, hornbeam, and lime, it pays playful homage to the chinoiserie beloved of the baroque era while also providing a delightful setting for string quartets.

The Jardin Rouge (Red Garden), with its scarlet flowers in pots, acts as an outdoor extension to the red salon in the house, which is known as Le Bâtiment. The Jardin Américain (American Garden) pays tribute to Christie's roots with over sixty species of plants native to North America. The Allée de Noisetiers (Hazelnut Alley), reached through a rocaille rustic archway, is lined with wood anemones, scillas, and miniature daffodils in spring, and offers a glimpse of the sixteenth-century dovecote, salvaged and rebuilt stone by stone. The vegetable garden and orchard fulfil the garden's essential function, in Christie's view, of nourishing both mind and body; he loves growing, harvesting, and cooking the vegetables for the gastronomic pleasure of his guests.

Le Bâtiment—a seventeenth-century bourgeois dwelling that was used as a farmhouse—has been restored throughout in keeping with the rural architecture of the Vendée region and is now listed as a historic monument. In the words of the Fondation Les Arts Florissants, "it allows young artists from all over the world to come and nourish their inspiration by frequenting a way of life that is permeated by the 'baroque spirit' to which William Christie has dedicated his life." •

The baroque spirit

♥ *Every summer, the Fondation Les Arts Florissants, founded by William Christie, and the département of the Vendée offer a week of music and discovery in the gardens, with more than a hundred events, from workshops, concerts, and musical walks to a variety of other encounters in this enchanting setting.*

Practical Information

Jardins de William Christie
32 Route de Sainte-Hermine
85210 Thiré
Tel.: +33 (0)6 86 80 67 37

Opening Hours

➻ Mid-March–end July and mid-September–late September:
Wednesday–Sunday (including public holidays, except May 1): 10:30 a.m.–5:30 p.m.

➻ August–mid-September and late September–mid-March:
Annual closure

➻ Final admissions one hour before closing

➻ **arts-florissants.org/en/jardins-patrimoine/les-jardins-de-william-christie**

Provence-Alpes-Côte d'Azur

Domaine du Rayol – Jardin des Méditerranées, Rayol-Canadel-sur-Mer • Var

DOMAINE du Rayol

Jardin des MÉDITERRANÉES

✲ Rayol-Canadel-sur-Mer, Var

Designed by landscape architect Gilles Clément, the Domaine du Rayol (owned by the Conservatoire du Littoral) is a conservation area dedicated to plants from Mediterranean climates the world over. From the art deco villa there are breathtaking views all the way down to the blue waters of the Mediterranean Sea.

Is it the pink of the sky reflected in the blue of the sea that carries us off into a reverie of times past? Or the ocher façade, with its Greek friezes and brown shutters, looking out over the rocky coastline of the corniche? Or the terraces bathed in sunlight on a glorious summer's morning? Or the exuberant maquis in this unreal corner of the Riviera, devoid of any concrete or artifice? It feels as though we are in a novel by F. Scott Fitzgerald, with Nicole and Dick, the glamorous but doomed central couple in *Tender Is the Night*, walking on the golden sands of the little cove beneath the art deco villa, with cypress trees rising into the azure sky and cicadas trying in vain to distract those two tormented souls. But we need to go back to before the Jazz Age, to the Belle Époque, to witness the birth of the Domaine du Rayol.

It was at this period that wealthy visitors such as the Eiffel and Royce families happened upon the magical, unspoiled shoreline of the Corniche des Maures. They lost no time in building their summer villas there, looking out to sea amid the rockroses and strawberry trees. Among them was Alfred Courmes—a prosperous businessman, extensive traveler, and amateur botanist forever in search of rare plants—who bought an empty plot of land on this coast, not far from a charming little fishing

Aucun engrais ou
pesticides de synthèse
n'est utilisé durant
phase de croissance
5,50

village called Saint-Tropez. He built a farmhouse, designed by the architect Guillaume Tronchet, and stables, adding a pergola designed by the landscape architect Ferdinand Bac after World War I. After building a second villa, he sold the main building in 1925, which was then turned into a hotel.

The years passed, and the hotel, which had become a casino, closed in turn. In the 1970s, a series of developers hatched plans to make it a tourist and party destination, but always met with stiff opposition from local governments and residents: it is to their determination that we owe the estate's miraculous survival. In 1989, the Conservatoire du Littoral bought the historic fifty-acre (twenty-hectare) estate, restored the buildings, and entrusted the overgrown garden to the landscape architect Gilles Clément.

Clément believes in the concept of the "planetary garden," reminding us of our dependence on the earth and our obligation to care for it. Wanting to highlight the fruitful cross-pollination of species from all over the world, and an awareness of the limits of biological resources, he created a garden that is an invitation to travel through Mediterranean landscapes from across the globe, each with a community of plant and animal species adapted to hot, dry summers and mild, rainy winters. Mediterranean landscapes are also juxtaposed with more arid or subtropical climates, in a series of lush displays over seventeen acres (seven hectares) celebrating the diversity and harmony between the flora of the northern and southern hemispheres.

Eleven gardens take us on a journey from the Canary Islands to California, from New Zealand to Chile, and from Subtropical America to the Jardin Marin (Marine Garden). First on the tour, revealing the diversity of the Mediterranean climate, is the garden representing a real landscape (as in all the gardens) from the Canary Islands, with a mild year-round climate that escaped the Ice Age and has preserved a flora that dates back to the Tertiary era. This accounts for the giant scale of many of the plants, including the giant asparagus and *Sonchus congestus*, which resembles a giant dandelion standing five feet (one hundred and fifty centimeters) tall. Coastal scrub and spurges form the first of the islands' landscapes, followed by landscapes characterized by tall dragon trees, and finally the high-altitude *pinar*, dominated by the Canary Islands pine, known for its resistance to fire, with seeds that can germinate in charred trunks after a fire.

The tropical vegetation of the Americas is represented in the Jardin d'Amérique Subtropicale (Subtropical America Garden), where plants from both the northern and the southern hemispheres—southern Mexico and Central America north of the

Equator and Argentina, Uruguay, Paraguay, and southern Brazil south of it—flourish together. The garden is watered constantly, which is essential for this tropical forest where you can see the *Tipuana tipu* tree with its bright yellow flowers, and erythrina, or coral tree, with its blood-red blooms. In this garden particularly, plants seed and spread themselves at will, with a freedom that is encouraged by the gardeners.

Finally, after a tour of Mediterranean climes and "planetary index" of their flora, including California, South Africa, Australia, Subtropical Asia, New Zealand, Arid America, and Chile, comes the Marine Garden. The final landscape at the Domaine du Rayol, this is an environment where nature is untouched by human hands. Visitors can learn about the sandy and rocky seabeds, the conger eel cave, the sea urchin beds, the mother-of-pearl passage, the Neptune grass meadow—a secret weapon in the battle against climate change that absorbs carbon dioxide in astounding quantities—and the unexpectedly important role of foreshore detritus. For those wanting to get up close to these wonders, there is even a marine tour, complete with flippers, mask, and snorkel.

More than just a series of beautiful gardens in a stunning setting, the Domaine du Rayol is a concept and a conservation area. It is a "planetary garden," a garden in constant evolution, and an exploration of the symbiotic relationship between humans and nature, and of how we can foster a way of living that respects our natural environment. In Gilles Clément's words, this is not a botanical garden, but a "land of nature and spirit." •

For a piece of the Med

♥ *Le Café des Jardiniers is open every day, except December 25, for lunch or a drink. On its terrace in the heart of the gardens, visitors can enjoy a culinary trip to the Mediterranean devised by chef Tom Ortin, using fresh, seasonal, and locally sourced produce. In addition, the ecological plant shop sells cuttings and seedlings from the estate's own nursery, and the gardeners' bookshop proposes over 4,000 titles in a comprehensive range of genres.*

Practical Information

Domaine du Rayol – Jardin des Méditerranées
Avenue Jacques-Chirac
83820 Rayol-Canadel-sur-Mer
Tel.: +33 (0)4 98 04 44 00

Opening Hours

Open daily throughout the year (including public holidays, except December 25):

- January–March and November–December:
9:30 a.m.–5:30 p.m.

- April–June and September:
9:30 a.m.–6:30 p.m.

- July–August:
9:30 a.m.–7:30 p.m.

- October:
9:30 a.m.–6:30 p.m.

- Final admissions one hour before closing.

- **domainedurayol.org/en**

Credits

t: top; b: bottom; l: left; r: right; c: center

Artists' Credits

© Adagp, Paris 2025 (Danielle Justes): p. 210 (t, bl); sculpture © Robert Arnoux: p. 129 (b); © Jean-Paul Moscovino, *RÉMANENCE*, folded BLUE on aluminum, h. 6 ft. 7 in. (2 m), MOSCOVINO / moscovino.com: p. 84 (t).

Photographic Credits

© Les Arts Florissants / Julien Gazeau: pp. 242, 244–245, 246, 250 (tl, tr, b); © Les Arts Florissants / Lionel Hug: pp. 248, 249 (t, b), 251; © aud781/ Shutterstock: p. 206; © Yann Avril / Biosphoto: p. 148 (tr, cr), 149, 150 (b); © Marie Aymerez / Biosphoto: p. 258 (cr); © Benoît Bacou / Photononstop: pp. 215, 216, 219, 220 (t, cl, cr), 221; © Olivier Benoist: back cover (br), pp. 12, 16 (t, b), 17; © BODY Philippe / hemis.fr: pp. 65, 70 (tl, tr, cl, b), 75, 84 (b), 85, 200 (b), 202 (tr), 226, 227; © BOISVIEUX Christophe / hemis.fr: p. 201 (tl); © BOUILLAND Stéphane / Hemis.fr: pp. 124, 127, 128, 129 (t, cl, cr), 130 (t, b), 131, 133, 136 (t, bl, br), 137, 138 (t, b), 139; © Charles Boulanger–Jardin Jungle: pp. 182, 183 (t), 184 (t, b), 185; © Michel Boulanger–Jardin Jungle: pp. 178, 181, 183 (bl, br); © Denis Bringard / Biosphoto: pp. 110 (t), 112 (t); © BRINGARD Denis / hemis.fr: pp. 109 (br), 110 (bl, br), 112 (b); © David Burton / Alamy / Hemis: pp. 40 (t, bl), 42 (br); © Dimitri Carol / Alamy / Hemis: pp. 205, 209; © Mahaux Charles / AGF Foto / Photononstop: pp. 37, 38, 40 (c, br), 41, 42 (tl, tr, bl), 43; © CHICUREL Arnaud / hemis.fr: pp. 57, 160; © CORMON Francis / hemis.fr: pp. 144, 146, 148 (tl); © DE LAGASNERIE / hemis.fr: pp. 200 (t), 201 (tr), 202 (tl, b); © Lionel Dominique: pp. 217, 218 (t, cr); © Philippe Dubreuil: pp. 171, 172, 173, 174 (t, bl, br), 175, 176 (t, b), 177; © Liz Eddison / Flora Press / Biosphoto: pp. 52 (b), 53; © ESCUDERO Patrick / hemis.fr: pp. 76, 84 (t), 201 (cr), 203, 228 (b), 229 (b), 233; © Guillaume Fandel: pp. 24, 25 (t); © Fotimageon / Shutterstock: p. 210 (bl); © FRILET Patrick / hemis.fr: p. 229 (cr); © GERAULT Gregory / hemis.fr: front cover, pp. 79, 150 (t, c); © Philippe Giraud / Biosphoto: p. 220 (b); © GIUGLIO Gil / hemis.fr: p. 71 (b); © Gérard JEAN: pp. 28, 30, 31, 33 (bl, br), 34 (t, b); © Lamontagne / Biosphoto: p. 106; © Gilles Le Scanff & Joëlle-Caroline Mayer / Biosphoto: pp. 109 (t), 156 (bl), 158 (tr), 159; © Alain Le Toquin / Biosphoto: pp. 145, 261; © Hervé Lenain / Flora Press / Biosphoto: pp. 46, 48, 49, 52 (t, cl, cr), 54 (tl, tr, c, b), 55; © LENAIN Hervé / hemis.fr: back cover (tc, bl), pp. 50, 58, 59, 64 (t), 70 (cr), 73, 78, 80–81, 82, 87, 88, 89, 90–91, 92 (t, cl, cr, b), 94 (l, r), 95, 96, 98–99, 101 (t, b), 102 (t, c, bl, br), 103, 117, 119, 120 (t, c, bl, br), 121, 122 (tl, tr, c, b), 123, 228 (t), 229 (t, cl), 232, 255, 259 (t), 262 (b); © LOURDEL Lionel / Hemis.fr: p. 187; © Stéphanie Madaule: p. 218 (cl, b); © MAMY Sébastien / Hemis.fr: back cover (bc), pp. 224, 230; © MAURICE Stéphane / Hemis.fr: pp. 163, 164, 165 (t, bl, br), 166–167, 169; © MOIRENC Camille / hemis.fr: pp. 257, 259 (b); © Yann Monel: p. 129 (b); © MORANDI Tuul and Bruno / hemis.fr: pp. 60–61, 62, 64 (b), 142, 148 (cl); © NICOLAS José / hemis.fr: p. 263; © NouN / Biosphoto: p. 63; © Luke Peters / Alamy / Hemis: p. 35; © Sibylle Pietrek / Flora Press / Biosphoto: pp. 198, 201 (cl, b); © PISTOLESI Andrea / hemis.fr: pp. 68, 71 (t); © PLANCHARD Eric / hemis.fr: p. 151; © Sylvie Patrick Quibel / le jardin plume: pp. 153, 154–155, 156 (t, c, br), 158 (tl, b); © RIEGER Bertrand / hemis.fr: pp. 188, 190 (t), 191, 192, 256, 258 (tr, cl, b), 262 (tl, tr); © Sabrina Rothe / Flora Press / Biosphoto: p. 113; © Éric Sander: back cover (tr), pp. 196, 235, 236, 237, 239, 240 (tl, tr, b), 241; © SCHMITT Franck/hemis.fr: p. 51; © Danièle Schneider / Photononstop: back cover (tl), pp. 67, 69, 74; © Florent Tanet: p. 26; © Nicolas Thibaut / Photononstop: pp. 190 (cl, cr, b), 193; © Daniel Thierry / Photononstop: pp. 21, 23, 25 (br), 33 (t); © Claude Thouvenin / Biosphoto: pp. 25 (bl, cr), 27; © Guy Thouvenin/robertharding/ Photononstop: p. 148 (b); © Frédéric Tournay / Biosphoto: p. 258 (tl); © manoj valavan arasu / Shutterstock: pp. 207, 210 (t, br), 211; © Jack Varlet: pp. 8, 10–11, 13, 15; © Jef Wodniack / Shutterstock: p. 109 (bl).

Editorial directors: Kate Mascaro and Julie Rouart

Editor: Helen Adedotun

Administration manager: Delphine Montagne

Design and illustrations (flowers): Amélie du Petit Thouars

Cover design: Audrey Sednaoui

Picture research: Marie Audet

Editorial collaboration: Florence Bott

Translation from the French: Barbara Mellor

Copyediting: Eleanor Corbett

Typesetting: Cathy Picns-Pays

Proofreading: Penelope Isaac

Production: Manon Pouch

Color separation: Graphium, Paris

Printed in Slovenia by DZS

Originally published in French as *Ma France des Jardins*

English-language edition

editions.flammarion.com
@flammarioninternational

26 27 28 3 2 1

ISBN: 978-2-08-049812-0

Legal Deposit: 03/2026

Flammarion is actively committed to reducing the ecological footprint of its publications. The book you hold in your hands was printed on paper made from wood sourced from sustainably managed forests, using vegetable-based inks, by a printer committed to environmental protection.